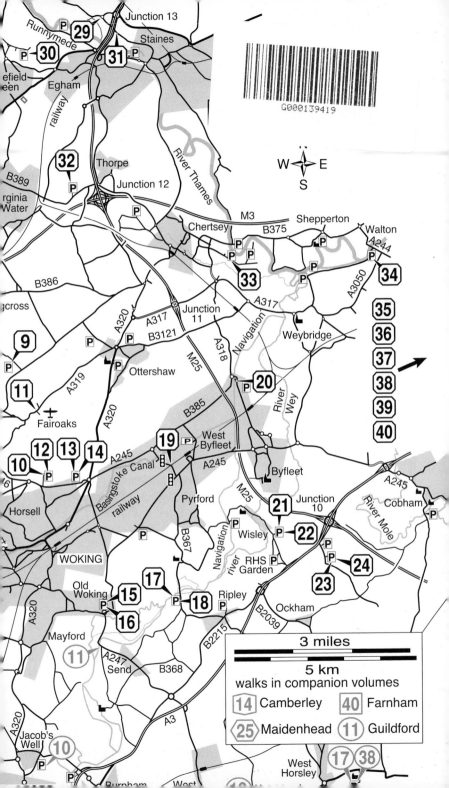

1 **West End, Brentmoor and Brook Place**

About 6½ km/4miles with a 1½ km/1 mile extension; heath and farmland.
OS maps 1:25000 160 Windsor, 1:50000 186 or 175.

Start from the village hall car park
at West End, SU 947 613. There is
also parking off Red Road near the
New England houses, SU 936 913.

Linking walks 2★ 5❖

Hare & Hounds ☎ 01276 858161

© Crown Copyright
MC 100011861

Bisley Brookwood Guildford

① From West End village hall
cross the village green to the
furthest corner (350m) and
continue on Streets Heath, the
road ahead (100m).

② Just after the main road (50m)
bear R on the footpath (120m). At
the hedge disregard the cross path
from the **Hare & Hounds** and the
R fork just after it, and carry on
beside the fields to the next road
(300m). Turn R and follow it round
L past the houses of Donkey Town
to the next road L (200m).

ⓔ *Extension of 1½ km/1 mile:
Turn L down the road to the end*
(300m) and stay ahead on the
footpath opposite between fields
then into a field (350m).

ⓕ *Pass round the bottom corner -*
not into the field below. ★ *Stay at*
the edge to the next hedge corner
(150m) and along the next field
(150m). Cross the footbridge.
Disregard side paths L and keep
on through the wood to end at a
hard track (250m).

ⓖ *Walk along the track R all the*
way to the lane (500m).

ⓗ *Go R on the lane (100m). At the*
R curve, take the track L up the
edge of the heath and round the L
bend (150m). ➔④

③ Keep on ahead skirting Donkey
Town (250m). After the last house
cross the ditch and carry on to the
boundary track (300m). Turn R.

④ Stay on the hard track up the
hill past the cross track from the
ranges just over the brow (400m).

2

⑤ After the cross track (30m) turn onto the next path R. Stay on it across Brentmoor Heath (400m).

⑥ At the end of the barrows L (lumps) bear R on the wide side path (30m) and fork R to the cross path up the brow of the hill (80m). Turn L. Go L over the rise, into the dip (100m) and up the track past the New England houses (200m).

⑦ Pass round the end of the last house, ½R and level, not steeply down. Stay on this track round a L bend (100m) to the end (250m). Go round the roundabout over the Guildford and Chobham roads (50m). Where the latter (Bagshot Road) leaves the roundabout take the footpath from the house drive under trees (150m) and diagonally over the sports field of Gordon's School to the wood near the L edge (200m). Walk on through the trees to the road (80m).

⑧ Go L down the road (100m) then R on the side lane (200m).

⑨ At the R bend turn L along the track between fields (150m). After the brook (the Mill Bourne) stay ahead on the path curving R through the wood (350m).

⑩ At the end turn R on the horse track between fields and woods. Stay on it to the road (650m). ❖

⑪ Go R on the road. Disregard L paths after Oakfield House (100m) and Roebuck Farm Cottage (300m) but join the track L at the R curve after the next house R (100m).

⑫ Follow the track beside the L fence and cross the farm bridge at the Mill Bourne (150m). Turn R on the other side then L up between the fields (100m). Halfway to the buildings cross the field diagonally L to the furthest corner (150m) and go out to the road (50m).

⑬ Cross and walk R along the verge past Brook Place (100m). Just after the entrance turn L on the footpath into the field, soon intersecting the branching drive (30m). Just into the R drive take the path beside the wall (50m). Stay ahead on the path (400m). At the houses continue on the un-made road to the end (200m). Turn R at the tarmac road but diverge L to the pond (30m) and carry on over the grass to the village hall.

The land of Chobham included West End and was given to Chertsey Abbey as part of its early endowments. This is known from the medieval copy of a charter of about 673 - one of the first Saxon documents to bring light to the Dark Ages. The abbey wielded great influence in the vicinity for 900 years.

By the end of the 7th century, charters accompanied royal grants of land. In them are recorded the place names of the areas given and boundary marks. People with their titles and positions appear as parties and witnesses to the transaction. The arrangements reveal custom and law, and the date.

The grant of 673 was by Frithuwold who refers to himself as sub-ruler of the province of Surrey under the king of Mercia. He mentions the abbey was built by King Egbert. The lands are Chertsey, Thorpe, Egham, Chobham, Molesey and Woodham, bounded on one side by the province of Sonning. Wulfhere, king of the Mercians, added his sign ✠ at Thame in confirmation.

This is the first record of Surrey and the other places named. It indicates Surrey was a protectorate of Mercia; at other times it was attached to the kingdoms of Kent or Wessex.

Early English Documents Vol 1 500-1042
Dorothy Whitlock 1955 Eyre & Spottiswood

2 Around Bisley

About 7 km/4½ miles through heath, pasture and woods with an extension of 1½ km/1 mile or a short cut of ½ mile. OS maps 1:25000 145 Guildford + 160 Windsor, 1:50000 175 Reading or 186 Aldershot.   Linking walks 1★ 3✳

Start from the car park on the village green at Bisley, SU 949 598. There is also a village car park opposite the south end of the village green, SU 949 595.

The Hen & Chickens ☎ 01483 473184   *The Fox* ☎ 01483 473175

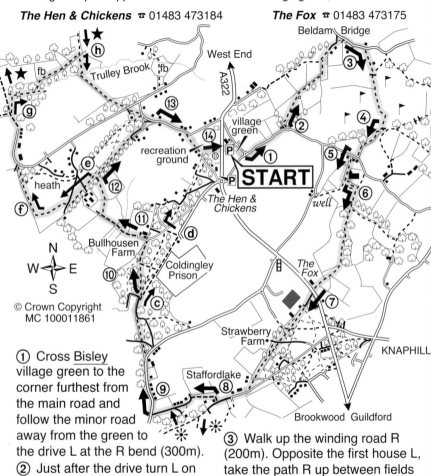

© Crown Copyright
MC 100011861

① Cross <u>Bisley</u> village green to the corner furthest from the main road and follow the minor road away from the green to the drive L at the R bend (300m).

② Just after the drive turn L on the footpath which bends R (50m). Stay on the main path converging on the adjacent fields L (200m) and follow it down the boundary into the field with the pond (200m). Turn L along the edge and join the path between fields (100m). Go R past houses and cut the corner R to the road near Beldam Bridge (200m).

③ Walk up the winding road R (200m). Opposite the first house L, take the path R up between fields (100m). Join the converging path and go on to the next track junction (400m).

④ Cross into the golf course R as far as the bridge (60m) then skirt the L edge (120m) and go down the next field to the road (80m).

⑤ Slightly R (30m) take the track L past Bisley Church (150m).

4

⑥ In the field after the churchyard go L along the hedge and out at the corner (100m). Follow the path R between the fields to the main road near the **Fox** (750m).

⑦ Cross and carry on along the track into Bisley Common (150m). Follow the R fence to the shed after the house (100m) then fork L but stay near the R boundary through the heath disregarding side paths (200m). Cross the drives of Strawberry Farm and Stafford Lake Farm (300m) to the pond (100m). Continue on the lane (R) until it bends L to the nursery (120m) then on the track ahead (100m). ✳

⑧ Take the side track R round the first house (200m). After the field R stay on the track L & R and past houses to the road (200m).

⑨ Turn R along the road past Bisley Ranges (400m). When it bends R follow the fence under the trees (300m) and the track ahead (150m). Just before the L bend, divert onto the path ahead.

ⓒ *½ mile cut: Don't fork L but stay on the straight track to the road at Coldingley Prison (500m).*

ⓓ *Turn L into the heath (100m). Turn R on the tarmac (30m) but after the side drive diverge on the path L. At the houses follow the garden boundaries ahead to the recreation ground (500m).* ✦⑭

⑩ Fork L immediately then L again (40m). Stay ahead on this path across the wood to Bullhousen Farm (350m).

⑪ Walk through the farm on the tarmac drive (70m), down the track between fields (150m) and up the L edge of the next field (100m). Halfway up bear R, cutting the corner to the stile R of the farm buildings (120m). Go straight over the next field (100m) and out into the heath.

ⓔ *Extension of 1½ km/1 mile: Just into the heath (40m), go L round the bend (40m) and over the farm drive. Carry on (150m) and cross the next drive. Swing L and R to the ranges fence (200m).*

ⓕ *Turn R and stay beside the fence to the lane (350m). Go L on the lane (300m), over the bridge and ahead on the track (100m).* ★

ⓖ *Opposite the side track L diverge R on the path under the trees to the T-junction (100m). Turn R through the wood (200m) and fork L to the footbridge (60m). Cross into the field and go R along the edge to the next field (150m) and ahead (150m).*

ⓗ *Just before the next hedge corner enter the field R and make for the bottom R corner (130m). Over the bridge (10m) turn into the field L and follow the R edge to the end (250m). Go on through the trees to the lane (120m). Just into the drive opposite, bear L across the wood (120m).* ✦⑬

⑫ Take the first R along the edge of the heath (400m). At the track continue ahead but fork R from the tarmac drive (200m).

⑬ At the road go R to the bend (350m) then walk out onto the recreation ground R. Either

⑭ cross the grass to the gateway at the middle of the main road edge to reach the village green (200m) or go out at the far end on the drive through the trees to the village car park (200m) and the **Hen & Chickens** (50m).

3 Pirbright and Brookwood Cemetery

About 8 km/5 miles with an extension of 1 km/¾ mile; along the Basingstoke Canal, over heath and through much of the the cemetery; fairly shady.
OS maps 1:25000 145 Guildford, 1:50000 186 Aldershot or 175 Reading.

Start from the village green car park at Pirbright, SU 946 561, or on the bank of the canal in Brookwood, SU 950 572.

The Brookwood Hotel ☎ 01483 472109   **The Cricketers** ☎ 01483 473198
The White Hart ☎ 01483 799715

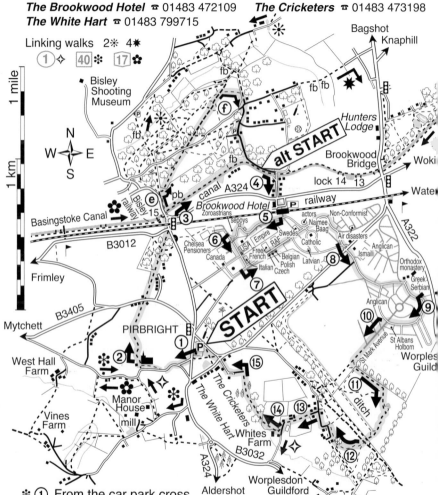

✳ ① From the car park cross the yard of Pirbright village hall to the main road (100m). Walk along the side road opposite (200m) then turn R into the graveyard. See the grave of Stanley (granite lump) and go on past the church to the path outside the churchyard (100m). ❀

② Turn R. Stay ahead between fields (400m), over the road and through trees to the road junction (500m). Go under the London to Southampton railway and ahead over the Basingstoke Canal bridge beside Lock 15 (100m).

(e) *Extension of 1 km/¾ mile: Go on to the L bend (100m). Turn R at the footpaths after two drives. ✳ Take the R path near the fence up into Sheets Heath (500m). Cross the lane and continue on the wide track past many side paths (500m).*
(f) *150m before the top end, take the path cutting across the corner R to the boundary trees (120m). Join the wide track and go R (60m), over a staggered 4-way junction ✳ and down to the canal (450m). Keep on to the bridge (200m). ↦(4)*

(3) Over the bridge drop R to the towpath and follow past a pillbox to the next bridge (900m).

(4) Cross the canal and walk up to Brookwood (200m), over the main road and up to the station (80m). Via the main door pass under it to Brookwood Cemetery (50m).

(5) Turn R along the drive parallel with the railway then winding past graves of Turkish airmen, sepoys to the Zoroastrians R (350m).

(6) Turn L downhill through the gate to the military area with ranks of Chelsea Pensioners R. Descend past Canadians R and Americans L to Long Avenue (300m).

(7) Turn L. Stay ahead on the straight (600m) then R round the Najmee Baag to the road (300m).

(8) Cross into the other part of the cemetery. Stay on the main tarmac drive to the fork at the Orthodox Church and Monastery (500m) then R past the Serbian Orthodox cemetery at the boundary (200m).

(9) Keep to the circular tarmac drive until it is crossed by the long straight St Mark's Avenue (400m).

(10) Go L along it, watching out for a path to the fence corner L (350m).

(11) Turn L into Brookwood Heath (40m). Follow the main path halfway along the L edge (250m) then ½R round the pond L and past the ditch R, to the fence (350m).

(12) Stay ahead over the boundary path of Pirbright Common and the track (20m) and along the narrow path (30m) then bear R on the side path winding towards the house (200m). Follow the boundary path R of the garden (150m). After the next house join the track L and follow it round bends (150m).

(13) At Whites Lane turn L (50m). Continue on the footpath (150m) and (L) on the next lane (50m). ◇

(14) Just before Whites Farm take the path R into the field (100m). Turn L but diverge from the edge to the far side 100m from the L corner (150m) and go on along the main path through the wood (300m).

(15) At the end of the path turn L along the nursery track and exit via the tarmac drive to the road beside the *Cricketers* (200m). Cross the green to the car park (200m).

Brookwood Cemetery was a private enterprise and is still privately owned though the military part now belongs to the nation. In 1850 the Burials Act proscribed burials at London churches. In 1851 the London Necropolis and National Mausoleum Company won an Act of Parliament to buy 2600 acres of Woking Common. The 400 acres furthest from Woking station became the cemetery and the rest was sold for building. The cemetery had its own train, branch line from the railway and London terminal. The peak year was 1866 with 3842 burials. Cremation was pioneered elsewhere at Woking and outstripped burials after 1986 but Islamic burials have given Brookwood Cemetery a new lease of life.

4 St John's to Brookwood Bridge

About 7 km/ 4¼ miles plus an extension of 2km/1½ miles; various short cuts possible; gently undulating and level beside the canal. OS maps: 1:25000 145 Guildford; 1:50000 186 Aldershot or 175 Reading.

Start from St John's village car park, SU 979 578.

Linking walks 3✱ 14✦

The Rowbarge ☎ 01483 761618
Hunters Lodge ☎ 01483 798101

① At St John's village car park cross the grass, away from the Memorial Hall, to the garden hedges (50m) and follow the path round between the trees and houses to the church (300m).

② Go past the church on the road (50m) but after the churchyard turn R down the side track (100m). When it forks to houses take the path from the R fork, over the footbridge (50m) and up through the trees to the bend in the lane at houses (100m). Cross the railway footbridge (30m).

ⓔ *Extension of 2 km/1½ miles: Keep on ahead to the clubhouse (70m) then follow the drive L down round the pond (80m) and up outside the golf course. Stay ahead to the 2nd road L (400m).*

ⓕ *Turn R beween the gardens and continue on the straight path across the fairways and through the trees to the next road (800m).*

ⓖ *Just along the road R (10m) turn R on the path beside the fence of Gorse Hill (100m). At the rear stay ahead under the trees and over a fairway to a track in the next trees (80m). Follow the track ahead to the club house (600m) then R & L to the railway (100m). Don't cross. Turn L.* ➔③

③ Take the path down beside the railway into the golf course (250m). Opposite the wood L diverge from the edge to pass through the end trees to a small stone footbridge (150m). Continue in a straight line, L of the reservoir, across belts of trees and fairways (500m) then beside fields, over a footbridge (150m) and up to buildings (200m). Go L to the road (100m).

8

④ Walk R along the road and down under the railway (600m).

⑤ Just after the tunnel (20m) turn R up the path to the Basingstoke Canal (80m). Go L on the towpath under Hermitage Bridge (200m) and all the way to the next road at Brookwood Bridge (1100m). ✷ *Lock 12 is just beyond the bridge. Over the bridge, a path behind the trees R of the road leads up past* **Hunters Lodge** *(250m).*

⑥ Follow the path back along the other side of the canal.

Ⓥ *Variant: A side path L (150m) leads up through grassland. At the first side path (80m) go R. Pass L of three ponds. Rejoin the canal. Continue beside the canal to the next road (1100m).*

⑦ Go along the pavement R and over Hermitage Bridge (100m). Join the towpath L and follow the canal round below the railway (London to Southampton line) to the canal footbridge (950m).

ⓐ *Alternative: Turn R on the path at the footbridge. Cross the lane and go on over a ditch (150m) and curve L along the railway (300m).*

ⓑ *At the football pitch L cross to the far corner (100m). Take the path under the trees, over a ditch to the cricket field (80m). Cross the grass to car park (150m).*

⑧ Stay on the towpath all the way to the next road at Kiln Bridge (500m). ✦ Turn R to the car park (100m) or past it and L along St John's Road to the **Rowbarge**.

The Domesday Book entry for Woking

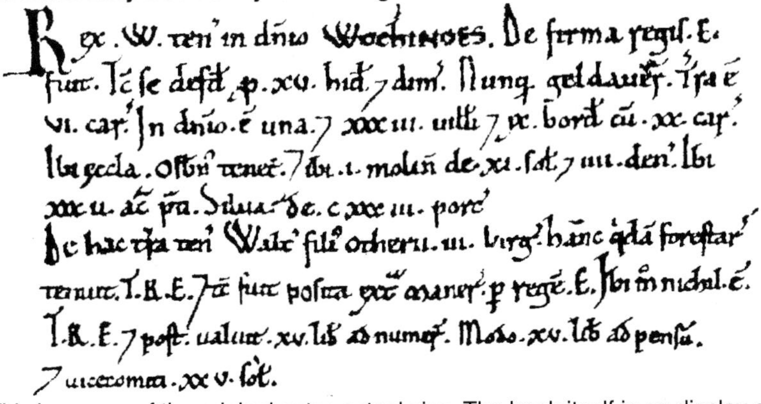

[handwritten Domesday Book Latin text, reproduced as facsimile]

This is a copy of the original entry, actual size. The book itself is on display at the National Archives in Kew. The R and the line through WOCHINGES are highlighted in red. TRE means in the Time of King *(Rex)* Edward ie before the Conquest. The entry is for the manor of Woking - an estate not a house or village. The survey was initiated at the Parliament of Gloucester in 1085.

King William holds in demesne WOCHINGES. Of king Edward's revenue it was. Then it was rated for 15 hides & a half; they never paid tax. Land for 6 ploughs. In demesne is 1; 33 villeins & 9 bordars with 20 ploughs. There is a church; Osbern holds it. There is 1 mill @ 11s 4d. There are 32 acres of pasture. Woodland @ 32 pigs.

Of this land Walter son of Othere holds 3 virgates. This a certain forester held TRE & then was put out of the manor by King Edward. Nothing there now. TRE & later value £15 at face value. Now £15 by weight / & to the sheriff 25s.

5 Chobham and Halebourne

About 7 km/4½ miles with an extension of 3½ km/2 miles to West End; mainly pasture land; lots of stiles. OS maps 1:25000 160 Windsor, 1:50000 175 or186.

Start from the village car park in Chobham, SU 974 6198, or park beside the green at Burrowhill near the *Four Horseshoes*, SU 970 629.

Linking walks 1❖ 7✹ 9✿ 10❂

The Hare & Hounds ☎ 01276 858161   **The Sun Inn** ☎ 01276 857112
The Four Horseshoes ☎ 01276 857581   **The Red Lion** ☎ 01276 858813

❂ ① In Chobham walk round L to the church (200m) and take the drive opposite, between the buildings, to the cemetery (120m). Stay ahead on the path (300m).
② At the field after the nursery go ½R on the path between houses (200m), L along the road (100m), R along Clappers Lane (120m) and round the L bend (80m).
③ After the house take the path R beside the brook, over the bridge and on (250m). Go L along the lane past houses (100m) and round to the end of the L field (200m).
④ Take the path L between fields (200m). At the end cross the brook into the field ahead and go straight over to the trees at the Mill Bourne (100m). Bear R. Stay beside the bourne to the bridge L (150m).
ⓔ *Extension of 3½ km/2 miles: Cross the bridge to the paddocks. Aim diagonally R from stile to stile (200m) then follow the hedge L into the next field (80m). Cross to the corner next to the garden and exit to the road (100m). Go R along the verge opposite (150m).*
ⓕ *Just after* Brook Place *turn L through the field (50m). Cross the side drive and go on along the track (50m). At the L bend stay ahead on the footpath (400m) then on the unmade road (200m).*

ⓖ *At the tarmac road in* West End, *go round the pond anticlockwise and along the L side of the village green to the corner (350m) then ahead on the roads (100m).*
ⓗ *After the main road (50m) take the path ½R (250m). At the hedge cross the path from the* **Hare & Hounds** ❖ *and fork R just after it. Carry on (200m) then turn R up the boundary path to the track on top (120m) (view 30m L).*
ⓘ *Follow the track R to the end (250m) and go round the roundabout anti-clockwise over two roads (50m). Where the road to Chobham leaves the roundabout take the footpath from the drive. After the trees (150m) cross the sports field of* Gordon's School *diagonally towards the L edge (200m) and go on through the trees (100m).*
ⓙ *Walk L down the road (100m) and R on the side lane (200m).*
ⓚ *At the R bend turn L along the track between the fields (150m). After the brook (Mill Bourne) stay*

ahead on the curving path through the wood (350m).

① *At the end, go R on the horse track between fields and woods all the way to the road (650m). Turn R along the road to the footpath L (100m).* ➤⑦

⑨ At the end of the garden (40m) turn L between gardens and fields up to the next lane (350m).

⑩ Walk down the lane R to the main road (900m) and R to the green at Burrowhill ✳ and the **Four Horseshoes** (200m).

⑤ Don't cross but keep on near the stream (100m) then turn into the next field L (after the stream bends L)(150m). Cross the fields diagonally to the hedge corner far R (200m). Follow the track out to the road (200m).

⑥ Go R along the road to the path R after Halebourne House (300m).

⑦ Take the path beside the track into the wood (150m). Go L under the trees and round the next corner of the wood (80m) then diverge from the wood across the polo field to the footbridge 60m from the corner (100m). Cross and make for the footbridge slightly L opposite (200m). Go along the L edge of the nursery on tracks and path until near the house. Cross the ditch L to get to the road R (300m).

⑧ Walk R on the road watching out for Steep Acre Farm L (300m).

⑪ Cross the main road halfway along the triangular green and take the path up the grass, not the main one but the little path diverging R from it. Stay ahead past the end of an unmade road R (200m). Keep on in the same direction on the unmade road R of Holly Cottage, to the field hedge L (150m).

⑫ Turn R to the **Red Lion** (70m). Opposite the pub go down the un-made road (80m). Stay ahead on the path (80m), over an u-m road and along the path (60m), past the end of the tarmac, ✿ along an u-m road (100m) and path (100m).

⑬ At the next road turn R (50m) then take the footpath L between the houses. Keep on to the end of the path (400m) then follow the pavement L to the Chobham village car park (200m).

6 Brick Hill and Chobham Common

About 7 km/4½ miles through heath and woods. Many circular walks can be made on the heath. This zigzag route is an introduction to the Common passing via the nicest places, the best landmarks and several car parks. Allow time for getting lost. OS maps 1:25000 160 Windsor, 1:50000 175 Reading.

Start from the car park at Chobham Place Wood, SU 964 642, or from Longcross Car Park, SU 979 651, or from Monument Car Park, SU 964 644.

Linking walks   7☆   9★

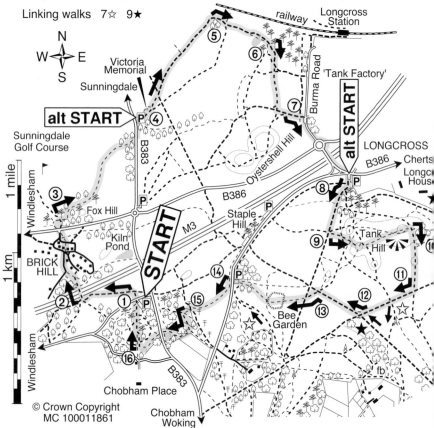

① At Chobham Place Wood cross the road from the car park. Go over the grass (30m) then turn L on the path. Keep on to the motorway footbridge R (400m).

② Cross (100m). Continue ahead through the trees (50m) then fork L to the houses of Brick Hill (100m). On the first (unmade) road go R, round the bend up to the T-junction (150m) and ahead on the path between the houses (70m). Cross the next road and stay ahead on the path to the main road (100m).

③ Cross slightly R and take the path into the trees (70m). Turn R on the cross path which bends L then curves R up behind the top of Fox Hill R (100m). Stay ahead on the narrow undulating path to the road (600m). Cross to the pavement and turn L to the car park (100m).

④ From Monument Car Park go up the main track to the fork (80m). Turn back L to see the Victoria Memorial (50m) then take the L track from the fork to the 4-way junction (100m) and ahead almost straight along the high heath ridge of Chobham Common (600m).

⑤ Carry on round the bend R and down into a valley (400m).

⑥ Go up the other side, curving R over the brow (100m). Descend to the track fork (150m) then stay ahead on the lesser path to the next major cross track (300m).

⑦ Turn L to Burma Road (200m) and walk up it R (200m). Keep on ahead, L of the roundabout, over the motorway then round L to the junction and car park R (300m).

⑧ At Longcross Car Park follow the main track away from the road disregarding the first side track R. At the little rise (100m) fork R down into Chobham Common (300m).

⑨ After the first bulge of Tank Hill turn L and make for the knoll on top of the second bulge (200m). Look along the hill rising from the knolls. Take the narrow path which leads to the highest point (350m). ★ ⚞⚟

Southwards the obtruding office block is in Woking. The long level ridge on the skyline is the North Downs with a V-shaped notch at Guildford where the River Wey cuts through. When the light is right the cathedral is visible.

⑩ Just over the high point (50m) turn R on the cross path and descend to the wide horse track before the power lines (350m).

⑪ Turn R, parallel with the power lines. Disregard the first major cross path (150m) ☆ and continue to the next which is oblique (250m).

⑫ Turn R again. Stay on this track to the oblique cross track (300m).

⑬ Bear L (100m). Cross the wide track and go straight on over the heath to the ring mound - the Bee Garden (150m). Keep on, curving R to the far side of the ring (100m). Bear R not on the path along the mound but on the rising path, briefly very steep. Stay ahead up to Jubilee Mount car park (250m).

⑭ Over the road from the car park find a gap to the heath. Walk L beside the road briefly (40m) then diverge from it. Make ½R for the wooded hilltop. The paths have largely disappeared. Aim for the highest part and join the path up the edge of the wood (300m).

⑮ At the bend in the path next to the highest electricity pole take the little path into the wood, over a boundary mound up to the ridge (50m). Bear R briefly on the ridge (20m) then take the side path L down through the trees to the corner of the field (150m). Turn R on the path outside the field (100m). At the next field bear R to the pond and go round R of it to the road (150m). Cross the road slightly L and climb the bank into the wood. Follow the path away from the road near the L boundary mound until just past another pond (200m).

⑯ Opposite Chobham Place (the house L over the road) turn R on the straight path through Chobham Place Wood to the car park (300m).

Brick Hill derives from the scatter of houses for workers of nearby claypits. Brick making started around 1750. By 1860 Woking was rapidly expanding and six companies were at work. The clay is part of the Bagshot Sands.

7 Burrowhill Green and Chobham Common

About 7½ km/4½ miles over heath with an extension of 1½ km/1 mile;
undulating; muddy and prickly in winter; sandy and prickly in summer.
OS maps 1:25000 160 Windsor, 1:50000 175 Reading.

Start from the green at Burrowhill, parking at the roadside near the *The Four
Horseshoes*, SU 970 629, or from Longcross Car Park, SU 979 651.

Linking walks   5✳ 6☆ 8❄ 9✦   ***The Red Lion*** ☎ 01276 858813
The Four Horseshoes ☎ 01276 857581

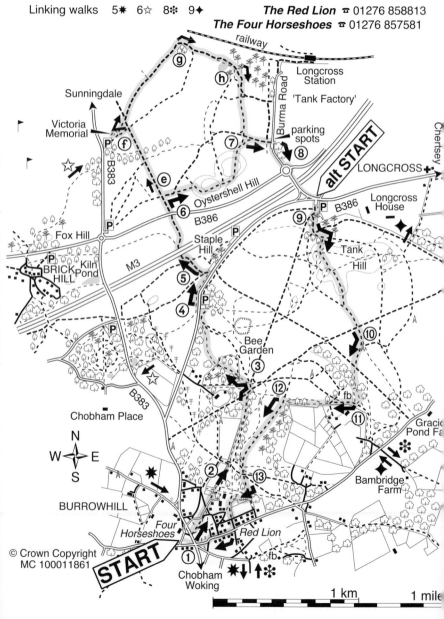

© Crown Copyright
MC 100011861

N
W ✦ E
S

1 km   1 mile

① From the **Four Horseshoes**, cross to the main road halfway along the triangular green and take the main path up the grass on the other side (150m). At the top join the tarmac lane ahead (100m).

② At the bend go on ahead under the trees, soon beside fields. At the end of the fields (600m) stay ahead to the wide path after the power cables (200m).

③ Go R (30m) then up the 1st L to the fork (50m). Turn L on the small path L which curves R up into the Jubilee Mount enclosure (80m). Go straight on (150m), out at the top and ahead through the heath to Jubilee Mount car park (400m). ☆

④ Find a gap to the heath on the other side of the road and go R beside the road (250m).

⑤ Just before the car park take the curving path L down under the motorway (200m). Follow the main track ahead (300m), over the next road to a cross path (150m).

ⓔ *Extension of 1½ km/1 mile: Stay on the same path into the valley and up to the cross path on the brow (500m).*

ⓕ *Turn L to the Y-junction (80m). Don't continue down the track to the car park but take the little path R to the memorial (30m). Return to the track junction (30m) and walk away on the other track (ie fork L) to a 4-way junction (100m). Stay ahead along the ridge (600m).*

ⓖ *Keep on round the R curve down into the valley (400m).*

ⓗ *Go up the other side, curving R over the brow (200m). Disregard the oblique cross path and continue ahead to a major cross track (300m). Turn L.* ✦⑦

⑥ Go R to the bend (100m) then take the path up Oystershell Hill and skirt R round the top (200m). Don't take the next L but carry on and curve L down the other side to the cross path (300m). Turn R.

⑦ Stay on the wide path to Burma Road (200m).

⑧ Walk up Burma Road R to the roundabout (200m). Stay ahead, L of the roundabout, over the M3 and round L to the junction and car park R (300m).

⑨ From Longcross Car Park follow the main track away from the road (100m) and fork L (100m). Go round the bend but don't diverge L on the horse track. Carry on (70m) and take the side path R on Tank Hill. ✦ Stay ahead past the first knoll R and the second knoll R (200m) and down a spur of the hill to the wide straight sandy track before the power lines (450m).

⑩ Continue ahead curving R to a pylon (100m). Skirt R of the pylon. and go on, across a wide path (150m). Follow the overgrown path down beside the wood (150m). Watch out for the stream in the wood R (30m) and follow it down (L) to the footbridge outside the riding school fields (100m). ✳

⑪ Cross the bridge and continue in trees outside the fields (500m).

⑫ Just after the last field turn L on the heath path. Disregard all side paths and the cross track (550m) and continue to the field R with a large boundary mound (200m).

⑬ Skirt R round the mound to the houses (200m) and go on to the road at the **Red Lion** (80m) ✳ then R to Burrowhill Green (300m).

8 Chobham, Fishpool and Fairoaks Aerodrome

About 9½ km/5¾ miles over fields and through the village. Impassable in wet seasons at ② when the alternative route (of equal length) is less muddy. OS maps 1:25000 160 Windsor, 1:50000 186 Aldershot.

Start from the village car park at Chobham, SU 974 619. Fishpool car park, SU 994 635, is close to the walk route.

Linking 5✿ 7❉ 9✹ 10❀ 11✿ 13✧

The Sun Inn ☎ 01276 857112
Blubeckers ☎ 01276 857580
Hanger Café at Fairoaks
   ☎ 01276 855446

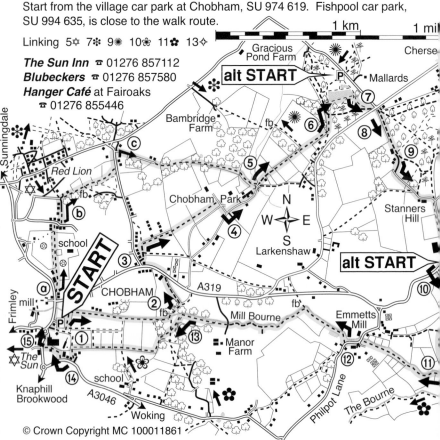

© Crown Copyright MC 100011861

① Behind <u>Chobham</u> car park, go L in the meadow to the stream (Mill Bourne) (200m) then R beside it. Disregard private footbridges from gardens but watch out for a public footbridge L just before a protruding bend in the R hedge (700m).

② Cross and follow the line of trees away from the stream (50m) then bear L along the R edge to join the road near the barn (200m). Follow the verge L (100m) and turn R into Mincing Lane (30m).

③ Take the track R after the corner house and up behind the gardens (120m). Disregard the first footpath R but take the second, along the top edge of the 2nd field. Go straight on over subsequent fields and down towards the large house, Chobham Park (600m).

④ Outside the last field go R on tarmac track over the first drive to the second (80m). Go L, past the farmhouse R and stables L and ahead over the bridge (300m).

⑤ Take the track L of the house to the fields and carry on along the L edges (400m). ✳ After the little wood L, stay ahead over the field to the corner (250m).

⑥ In the wood, follow the track L along the boundary (200m). Watch out for the <u>fishpond</u> R and take the path beside it to the end (200m). Fishpool car park is L from the end (100m) but if continuing turn R. ➔⑦ If starting from Fishpool Car Park face the road and take the path R down between the fishponds (100m) and ahead.

⑦ Stay ahead on one of the small paths to the track then L to the road junction (250m). ✧

⑧ At the tracks opposite take the R path up next to the field (400m).

⑨ At the house go R to the drive. Follow it L past the large house, Stanners Hill (250m) to a junction and on down (shady path at side) to the road (500m).

⑩ Walk along the verge R (100m) then follow the Youngstroat Lane into <u>Fairoaks Aerodrome</u> (150m). Stay ahead on the path beside fields past the runway (500m). The large house far L beyond the aerodrome is <u>Ottershaw Park</u>. ❀❀

⑪ Immediately after the stream (Mill Bourne) turn R along the bank. Stay on the bank, outside the fields, to <u>Emmetts Mill</u> (600m). Continue ahead on the road (150m).

⑫ Round the S bend, before the house R, take the footpath R over the footbridges (70m) and keep on round the bend beside the stream, soon in a field. Disregard bridges R (300m) and carry on beside the stream (700m). Cross the drive of Manor Farm. Soon after it (80m)

cross a hedge which diverges L but stay near the stream (300m).

⑬ When the L hedge bends L, cut across the grass diagonally L or go round the L edge to the furthest hedge corner (not into the field L) (200m). Pass into the next meadow and follow the L edge round the corner (100m). Keep to the L edge all the way to the path outside the cricket field at Chobham (600m).

⑭ Go L between the houses to the road (80m) then R (80m). Turn R on the path after the village hall to the churchyard and rejoin the road opposite the ***Sun*** (200m). ✿

⑮ Follow the road R through the village past ***Blubeckers*** and R at the junction (150m). The 1st & 2nd R turns lead to the village car park.

ⓐ *Alternative: On the main road outside Chobham village car park go R to the road junction (120m). Just after it, at the grass (50m), diverge R on the footpath, soon between sports fields (400m).*

ⓑ *At the housing estate go R on the road (50m) then take the path L between the houses and carry on along the (unmade) road to the T-junction (150m). ✳ Turn R on the path under the trees (Little Heath) (150m). At the bridge don't fork R but keep on to the road (250m).*

ⓒ *Go L on the road (120m). Just before the bend turn back R along the drive to Worlds End Cottage (250m). Continue on the footpath ahead under the trees (600m). At the end of the wood follow the stream (80m) and cross the footbridge to the corner of the field at the track below the house (50m). Turn L. ➔⑤*

9 Fishpool, Chobham Common and Longcross

About 6½ km/4 miles with a 1 km/¾ mile extension; over confusing heath and the Longcross lawns; undulating, boggy at ⑯ in wet seasons.
OS maps 1:25000 160 Windsor, 1:50000 175 Reading.

Start from Fishpool car park on Gracious Pond Road, SU 994 635.

Linking walks 6★ 7✦ 8✳ 11✪ 13❖

The Four Horseshoes ☎ 01276 857581   **The Red Lion** ☎ 01276 858813

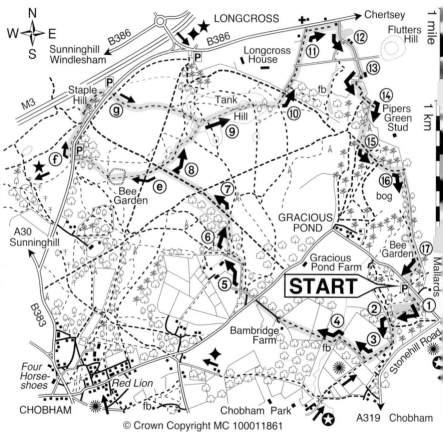

© Crown Copyright MC 100011861

✳❖✪ ① Facing the road take the path R from the car park down between fishponds (100m). Turn R along the long pond and stay ahead to the boundary (200m).

② Follow the boundary track L (200m) and turn R into the corner of the field. Go straight on beside the fence then over the field to the corner of the wood (200m). ✦

③ Turn R up the edge of the field beside the wood (250m).

④ Go L round the top corner of the wood (50m) then R over the footbridge. Carry on up between the fields (400m) and out along the farm drive (150m). Cross Gracious Pond Lane and go along the riding school drive opposite, almost to the house L (120m).

18

⑤ Turn R along the path outside the field (200m) - the boundary of Chobham Common. Join the track round the corner of the field L to the horse bridge (100m).

⑥ Don't cross the stream but turn R beside it (100m) then R again to the path outside the trees (20m) and L up to the wide heath track which crosses obliquely (150m).

⑦ Go L on the track, under the power cables (200m) and over a rise to a wide cross track (200m). *Look ahead. A lumpy ridge curves round on both sides. The route is onto the R arm of the ridge, Tank Hill, and along it. The extended route goes to the L arm first.* Stay on the track ahead (300m). Turn off at the oblique cross path (100m before the next major track).

★ⓔ *Extension of 1 km/¾ mile: Bear L to the wide track (100m) and go straight on over the heath to the ring mound - the Bee Garden (150m). Keep on, curving R to the far edge of the ring (100m). Bear R on the path up the slope. Stay ahead, briefly very steep, to Jubilee Mount car park (250m).*

ⓕ *Over the road find a gap to the heath and walk R beside the road (300m). Carry on past the car park and find a path up L in the pines to Staple Hill. Stay on the ridge to the exit of the next car park (250m).*

ⓖ *Cross the road and go straight down through the heath (400m), over the wide track and up onto the R knoll of Tank Hill (200m).* ➜⑨

⑧ Take the path back R up round the flank of a small hill L and fork R on one of the steeper paths to the knoll on top of the first spur of Tank Hill (500m).

⑨ From the knoll, look along the rising ridge and take the path which leads to the highest point (350m). Just after the top is a cross path (50m). Slightly R (15m) take the small onward path down the end of the hill to a 4-way junction (200m).

⑩ Stay ahead down to the boundary track (80m) where a path passes through the fence to the wood. Go through the wood (100m) and on along the L fence, over the drive of Longcross House (100m) almost to the road near Longcross Church (100m).

⑪ Walk R along the edge of the park near the road (300m).

⑫ From the main gates take the drive back across the park, round L after the pond and over crossroads to the next buildings (350m).

⑬ Bear R to the wood (70m) and go on along the winding horse track in the trees (200m). Don't take the wide branch track R.

⑭ At the next gateway go R along the fence (100m). When the fence bends L, continue ahead, L of the barrow (100m), under the power cables (100m) and down to the next crossing track (70m).

⑮ Turn L down the track (200m). When it bends R, continue ahead on the footpath curving L to the boundary mound & ditch (200m).

⑯ Don't cross the boundary. Turn R and pick your way through the thicket keeping near the boundary ditch and eventually joining the path ahead past the lesser Bee Garden (concealed by bracken in summer) (400m). Keep on along the boundary path (200m).

⑰ On a little rise the path bends R to the road and car park (200m).

10 Horsell Common, Chobham & Emmetts Mill

About 8 km/5 miles with a short cut of 2½ km/1½ miles; over fields and heath.
OS maps 1:25000 160 Windsor, 1:50000 186 Aldershot.

Start from the western car park on Horsell Common, TQ 001 604, or from the village car park in Chobham, SU 974 619.

Linking walks 5✪ 8✿ 11✾ 12✳ 13☆ 14✪

The Sun Inn ☎ 01276 857112   **Blubeckers** ☎ 01276 857580

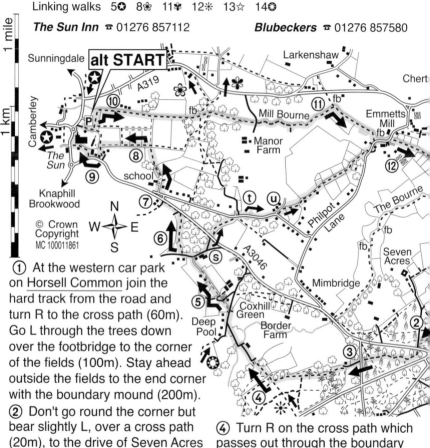

① At the western car park on Horsell Common join the hard track from the road and turn R to the cross path (60m). Go L through the trees down over the footbridge to the corner of the fields (100m). Stay ahead outside the fields to the end corner with the boundary mound (200m).

② Don't go round the corner but bear slightly L, over a cross path (20m), to the drive of Seven Acres (150m) then L to the road (60m). Opposite, take the horse track into the trees. It curves R, parallel with the next road (100m), then bends away from it, winding across the Common to another road (300m).

③ Cross and go along the drive opposite to Bourne Place (100m). Continue past the house on the horse track through the Common disregarding all side paths (500m).

④ Turn R on the cross path which passes out through the boundary nearby (40m). Carry on between fields (100m). Stay ahead on the track, round the S-bend over the stream (Bourne) (200m) to houses (150m) then bear R (100m).

⑤ After the 2nd house turn L into the nursery at the field gate and follow the R hedge (100m). The nursery plots disrupt the line of the right of way and it is best to turn L to the parallel hedge then R to the track outside the nursery (50m). Over the track, slightly R, the path resumes the original line between the fields (200m). At the houses (Milford Farm) keep on to the end of the tarmac drive (150m).

Ⓢ *Short cut of 2½ km/1½ miles: Go R on the unmade road (100m). At the large house, fork L to the road (100m). Cross to the horse track opposite and carry on through the trees to the next road (250m).*

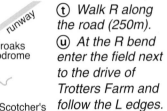

Ⓣ *Walk R along the road (250m).*

Ⓤ *At the R bend enter the field next to the drive of Trotters Farm and follow the L edges. round to a house R (200m). Skirt the gardens ahead (150m) and bear R across the next field (150m). Over the track continue ahead through a paddock to the far corner (200m). Join the road and go L to the bridge (200m).* ➔⑫

⑥ Turn L (60m). Between the first & second houses L watch out for the path R through the trees and follow it to the road (300m).

⑦ Walk along the pavement L to the road junction (100m) and cross to cul-de-sac part of the side road. Just after the junction (50m) turn R on the tarmac drive at the edge of the school site (100m). Carry on along the edge of the sports area (100m) and across the middle of the next field (100m).

⑧ In the next field turn L. Keep to the edge of the meadows all the way to the path outside the cricket field at Chobham (300m).

⑨ Turn L between houses to the road (80m) then R (80m). After the village hall take the path R to the church, rejoining the road opposite the **Sun** (200m). ❷ Go R through the village past **Blubeckers**. At the road junction (150m) turn R. Take the 1st R to the car park (100m). ✾

⑩ In the meadows behind the village car park go L to the stream, Mill Bourne (200m), and R beside it. Disregard a footbridge L near the bend of the R hedge (700m) ✿ and carry on (400m). Cross the drive of Manor Farm and continue beside the stream (550m).

⑪ Follow the R bend in the stream and cross footbridges to the road (350m). Go L on the road round the S-bend to the bridge (150m).

⑫ Don't cross the road bridge at Emmetts Mill but turn R beside it and continue on the bank of the Mill Bourne to the horse track from the bridge (600m). ☆ Ottershaw Park is the grand house visible beyond Fairoaks Aerodrome.

⑬ Turn R and cross the next stream (the Bourne) (150m). Stay on the path ahead to the vehicle track at the corner of Horsell Common (400m). ✳

⑭ Cross the track and bear L on the path through the heath to the tiny pond L (250m).

⑮ At the pond turn R (80m) then L on the cross path. Stay ahead to a cross path (200m) and bear R to the wide track and car park in the trees (200m). ❸

11 Fairoaks, the Bourne and Mimbridge

About 8 km/5 miles, mainly through meadows and woodland.
OS maps 1:25000 160 Windsor, 1:50000 186 Aldershot.

No large parking places. Use the spaces beside the A319 opposite Fairoaks
Aerodrome, TQ 001 624, or beside Sandpit Hall Lane, SU 984 613.

Linking walks 8✿ 9✪ 10✳ 12★ 13✽ 14✪

Hanger Café at Fairoaks 01276 855446

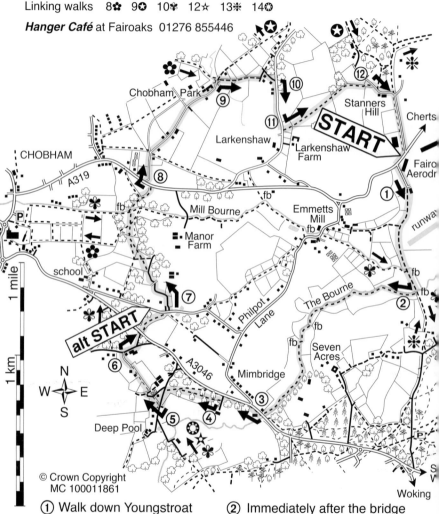

① Walk down Youngstroat
Lane beside Fairoaks Aerodrome
(150m). At the L bend stay ahead
on the path between fields.
Ottershaw Park is visible far L over
the runway (500m). ✳★✪ Cross
the first stream (Mill Bourne) and
carry on to the second (200m).

② Immediately after the bridge
turn R on the bank of the Bourne.
(This path was created by the
trustees of Horsell Common.)
Follow it from field to field (1000m)
then cross the footbridge. Continue
on the other bank along the field to
the road at Mimbridge (600m).

22

③ Cross the road and walk R along the pavement, past Philpot Lane (100m) and ahead (200m).

④ Turn L into the drive of Border Farm but watch out for the side path R in the trees (40m). Follow the path through the trees (300m). Join the converging path and carry on to the hard track near the nursery gateway (100m).

⑤ Turn L along the hard track to the first house R (120m). Just before the house turn R at the field gate into the nursery and follow the R hedge (100m). The nursery plots disrupt the line of the right of way and it is best to turn L to the parallel hedge then R to the wide track outside the nursery (50m). Over the track, slightly R, the path continues on the original line between fields (200m). At the houses (Milford Farm) keep on to the end of the drive (150m). ❧

⑥ Turn R along the unmade road (100m) and, at the large house, fork L to the road (100m). Cross to the path opposite and carry on under wires through the trees to the next road (250m).

⑦ Cross, slightly R. Take the drive of Manor Farm winding round past fields R (300m). Enter the corner of the first field L. Cross diagonally R towards the bulging corner of trees (150m). Go on in the same direction to the middle of the far edge under trees (100m). ❧ In the next field aim for the gap in the centre of the opposite edge (200m) or skirt R round the edge. Cross the foot bridge and follow the line of trees ahead (100m). Disregard a side path L and continue at the edge of the field to the road (200m).

⑧ Go L along the verge (50m) and cross into the drive of Chobham Park. At the fork (200m) stay on the main drive R to Chobham Park Farm (500m). Carry on past the stables L to the bridge (150m). ✪

⑨ After the bridge go R on the path along the garden hedge then between fields to the houses in the trees (300m). Follow the main track L & R to the road (200m).

⑩ Walk past the houses along the road R (300m). In the first small field L watch out for a path, 30m before the Larkenshaw drive.

⑪ Cross the little field into the larger one beyond (80m). Walkers tend to follow the L edge around but the right-of-way is straight across to the top edge at a point 30m from the L corner (300m). Continue ahead at the L edge of the next field past the trees and round R up towards the wood (250m). At the top corner exit to the tarmac drive (30m). ❋

⑫ Go down the drive R past the large house, Stanners Hill, to the drive junction (200m). Carry on down. There is a shady path R of the drive (400m). At the road turn R to the parking place.

Silver Birch has female catkins which become fruiting catkins, 3 cm long. The fruits are small and winged and drop like confetti in late summer to be blown great distances.

fruit x1

The word *birch* is evidently ancient for cognates are found throughout Indo-european languages: *bhurja* Sanskrit, *betula* Latin, *beith* Gaelic, *birke* German *bezuenn* Breton, *breźa* Old Slavonik, *berzas* Lithuanian but *koivu* in Finnish which is not Indo-european.

12 Horsell Common and Mimbridge

About 7 km/4½ miles; mainly through heath and woodland; flat; bridleways muddy in winter OS maps 1:25000 145 + 160, 1:50000 186 Aldershot.

Start from the western car park of Horsell Common, TQ 001 604.

Linking walks 10✼ 11★ 13✼ 14★

The Plough ☎ 01483 714105

① From Horsell Common west car park, go along the track towards the main road (100m). Halfway to the road, take the side path ½R and cross the road junction to Cheapside (100m). Follow the lane beside the trees. Stay ahead to the **Plough** (600m).

② Continue along the road L from the pub (150m) then diverge R on the path through the trees, across a side road. Stay ahead to the houses (200m) then along the tarmac drive (200m) then along the track to the R bend (100m).

③ Go on round the R bend to the main road (100m). Cross to Horsell Common and take the main path ahead to the far boundary (350m). Carry on between fences (100m). At the field join the track ahead and pass round the S-bend over the Bourne (200m) to the next houses at Deep Pool (150m). ✼★ Follow the track R past houses, into the trees (200m).

④ Just before the nursery drive L take the path R through the trees (100m) and fork R on the side path which ends at the drive of Border Farm (300m). Turn L to the road in Mimbridge (40m). Walk along the pavement R past the side road towards the Mim Bridge (300m). Cross the road near the bridge.

ⓐ *Shady alternative: After the Mim Bridge (40m) find the horse track under the trees L into Horsell Common. Diverge from the road to the drive of the farm (300m). Cross and go on along the track (200m). When it bends to the last house stay ahead on the path through the wood to another track - the drive of Seven Acres (150m).*

ⓑ *Turn L (30m) then fork R on the R hard track beside the field (120m). Opposite the house turn R. Disregard side turns and snake round several houses. After the fields join the perimeter track of Horsell Common (500m). Just along the hard track, from the bend L (30m) take the path R. ➜⑦*

⑤ Just before the bridge enter the field L and follow the bank of the Bourne to the end of the field (600m). Cross the footbridge and carry on along the bank from field to field to the horse track crossing the Bourne (1000m). ✼

⑥ Walk along the horse track R to the perimeter hard track at the corner of Horsell Common (400m). Cross to the path slightly L.

⑦ Follow the path into the heath (100m) and turn L on the first cross track staying near the edge of the Common to the fork (400m). Take

24

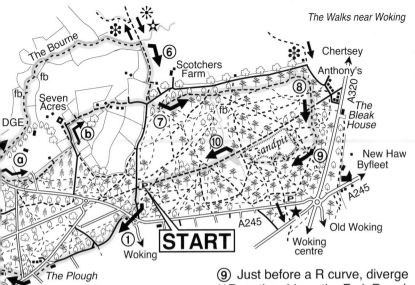

the L track to open heath and keep on near the L edge to the little pond L and the trees at the end (550m) then round R to a cross track (200m), near Anthony's (hamlet).

⑧ Go on under trees (120m) to another cross track. Stay ahead disregarding side paths (150m). ★

⑨ Just before a R curve, diverge ½R on the side path. Fork R and cross another path (100m) to the corner of the sandpit in the trees (20m). Go L all the way along outside the sandpit (650m).

⑩ At the far end of the sandpit, join the wide parallel straight track and carry on in the same direction, R of the pond, to Horsell Common west car park (600m).

Commons are usually open to the public for air and exercise but are not owned by the public or by the nation. They are remnants of land called *waste* in early documents which was not ploughed for crops but used for grazing, firewood, peat cutting, building materials, etc. As the population became denser the waste was divided between communities who marked boundaries with mounds or hedges in medieval times. The land now belonged to the lord of the manor and commoners; they could use it for themselves but not work it for private profit or sell it.

For enterprise there was a tendency from the Middle Ages onwards for shared arable land to be parcelled by agreement into private farms and much of the waste was taken up in the process. If commoners resisted, they were overcome, later on, by private Acts of Parliament. In general, only village greens and the least useful commons survived. Surrey has large commons because of poor soils and extensive heaths on the Tertiary (Bagshot) Sands and Lower Greensand.

In the 20th century commons lost sight of their commoners; a commoner might have the right to graze two cows but was not allowed to fence them and would not want to herd them; coal replaced peat and firewood; etc. By default, lords of the manor became the only visible owners and were able to dispose of commons. In Surrey they sold to boroughs, builders, the Army, preservation societies and the Forestry Commission. There are still a few commoners with registered rights.

The Common Lands of England & Wales   W G Hoskins & L Dudley Stamp 1963 Collins

13 Horsell Common and Fairoaks Aerodrome

About 8½ km/5¼ miles, around Fairoaks Aerodrome, through pinewoods and over heath with a 1 km/¾ mile extension. Horsell Common and Stanners Hill have numerous paths which can be explored but the route takes you via the main landmarks. OS maps 1:25000 160 + 145, 1:50000 186 Aldershot.

Start at Horsell Common main car park near Six Ways, TQ 011 603, or, on the extension, at Monument Lane car park, TQ 015 597.

Linking walks

8✧ 9❖ 10☆ 11❋ 12❉ 14✹ 19❉

Hanger Café at Fairoaks 01276 855446
Bleak House 01483 760613

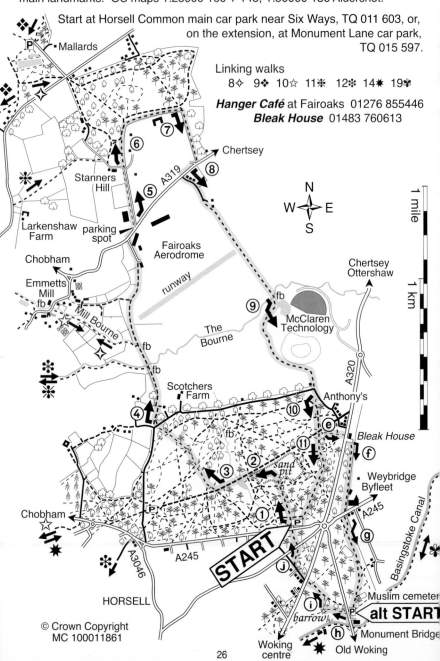

© Crown Copyright
MC 100011861

① Follow the footpath from the car park entrance straight over Horsell Common and into the sandpit (sometimes partly flooded) (400m).

② Turn L and make your way to the narrow end of the pit (200m). Outside join the parallel straight track and continue ahead, R of the pond (100m) and on (150m). ☆✳

③ Turn R on the first substantial cross path. Disregard the many side paths. Don't fork R (200m) but keep on past a tiny pond (200m) to the boundary track at the corner of the Common (250m).

④ Continue, opposite, on the soft bridleway over two streams, the Bourne (500m) ✳ and Mill Bourne (200m).✧ (The mansion visible far R across Fairoaks Aerodrome is Ottershaw Park.) At the end (500m) stay ahead on the drive (200m).

⑤ At the road go R (100m) then up the house drive L. A shady path runs beside it L (400m). ❖

⑥ At the fork after Stanyards Farm, take the path between the branches. Ascend under trees then make your way R to the boundary. Follow the path beside gardens across Stanners Hill and on outside the field R (700m).

⑦ At the end of the field take the path R beside it down to the road (350m). Go R on the road (200m).

⑧ Turn L on the track (Bonsey's Lane) at the houses. When it bends to the farm (250m) stay ahead on the path past the end of the runway and down to the Bourne (800m).

⑨ Over the footbridge, stay on the curving path past the McClaren building L, up round the hillock and down to the house at the edge of Horsell Common (900m).

⑩ Continue ahead (50m) then take the path through the trees R (50m) and turn L on the heath horse track. Pass over the first cross track (150m) and continue to the second (120m) near Anthony's. Either ⑪ Stay on the path ahead all the way to the car park (600m) *or* ⓔ *Extend the route by ¾ mile/ 1 km: At the 2nd cross track don't continue ahead but turn L to the next path junction (20m). Turn R (15m) then branch ½L straight to the road (traffic visible) and cross to the **Bleak House** (150m).*

ⓕ *From the pub car park take the path R along the boundary of the Common to cross the next road near Woodham Church (500m).*

ⓖ *Opposite, keep on along the path, curving R from the boundary (100m). On the crossing path from the road go L past the corner of the boundary mound R (200m). Just after the mound fork R. Join the converging path (100m) and go past the Muslim cemetery to the car park at the road (250m). Walk up onto the Monument Bridge over the Basingstoke Canal (50m). ✳✳*

ⓗ *Return along the pavement on the other side of the road looking for a path L opposite the car park but before the pylon (70m). Follow the path across the Common to the bell barrow (200m).*

ⓘ *Opposite the barrow find the path R in the trees and follow it to the long straight path (100m). Go L to the road (150m), across it and along Carlton Road to Woodham House (150m).*

ⓙ *Take the path R across two roads to the car park (250m).*

14 Woking and the Basingstoke Canal

About 9½ km/6 miles; woods and heath and along the towpath in Woking; very muddy in wet seasons. OS maps 1:25000 145+160, 1:50000 186 Aldershot.

Start from Horsell Common main car park near Six Ways, TQ 011 603, or the West car park, TQ 001 604, or from Littlewick Recreation Ground, SU 981 592.

Linking 4✦ 10✿ 11✿ 12★ 13✱ 19❀   **Fox & Flowerpot** 01483 228920
Bridge Barn 01483 763642

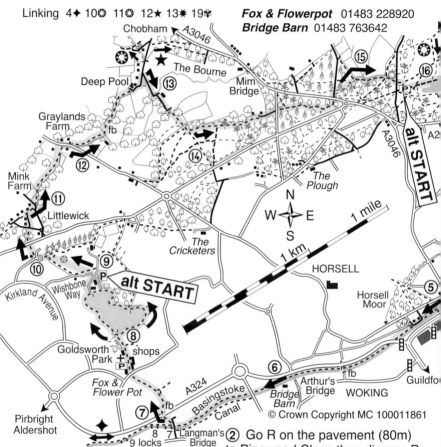

© Crown Copyright MC 100011861

① Near Six Ways take the path over the road from the car park exit, through <u>Horsell Common</u>, (100m). Cross the next road and go on to Woodham House (120m) then L to the main road (120m).

ⓔ *¼ mile extension: Cross. Go on through the trees (300m) and R on the road over the canal (120m).*

ⓕ *R from the bridge take the towpath to the next bridge (650m).* ✦④

② Go R on the pavement (80m) to Pinewood Close then diverge R on the path in the trees (150m).

③ After the next road (50m), bear L on the side path. Keep on over a ditch (150m) to the pond (200m) then climb to the road. Cross it and the <u>Basingstoke Canal</u> (100m).

④ At the end of the bridge drop L to the towpath (20m). Go under the bridge & on to the next road (500m).

⑤ Cross the canal and continue on the other side through <u>Woking</u>

28

(450m), under the next road and on to Arthur's Bridge near the **Bridge Barn** pub (700m).

⑥ Stay on the towpath, under the next road (300m) to the bridge at the first lock (No 7) (500m). ✦

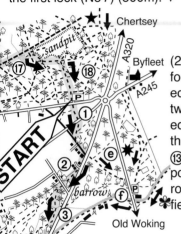

Chertsey

sandpit

A320

⑰ ⑱ Byfleet

A245

P ①

START

② e

barrow P f

③

Old Woking

④

⑦ Turn R, not down the track but up the diverging walkway over the road and ahead to the next road at Goldsworth Park (500m). Keep on ahead past the **Fox & Flowerpot**, along the shop fronts into the park and ahead to the pond (300m).

⑧ Follow the path round to the children's play area at the far end of the pond, L (500m) or R (600m).

⑨ Walk away from the pond past the buildings ★ and cut straight over the grass and football field into the far L corner (500m).

⑩ Exit L and cross the road circle (50m). Turn R along the walkway beside Weasdale Court to the main road (100m). Cross to the footpath in the trees. Keep on to the track (100m), then slightly L and along the side track to the end (100m).

⑪ Turn R along the garden hedges (80m). Cross the S-bend

at the next track (Mink Farm drive) to the field and continue along R edges in the trees to the large field (100m). Keep on to cross the bridge at the far R corner (200m) and go out to the road (100m).

⑫ Cross the road and turn R to the first field (50m). Follow the path round the R edge, soon diverging from the road (200m). Bear L across the next field to the footbridge (50m). Go straight over to the edge of the field (30m) and ahead between two fields (150m). In the next field follow the edge R to the corner (80m). Stay ahead on the track past the house (100m). ✿★

⑬ Turn back R on the side track past the pond to the Bourne bridge (150m). Keep on round the S-bend and along the edge of the field (150m). Don't turn L with the track but go out at the corner then between fences (150m) and into Horsell Common.

⑭ Start along the path ahead (40m) but take the cross path L at the edge of the heath and through the trees to Bourne Place (500m). Go on along the drive (100m), over the road and through the trees on the winding horse track (400m).

⑮ Cross the road and follow the hard track opposite (Seven Acres drive) (60m). At the cross path go R to the corner of the fields (200m). Stay ahead outside (R of) the fields to the next corner (200m) then bear R over the footbridge up to the hard track near the W car park (100m).

⑯ Walk through the car park and on along the broad track ✳ until past the pond R (700m).

⑰ Take the next path R and skirt round outside the sandpit (200m).

⑱ At the cross path from the second spur of the sandpit, turn R to the main car park (200m).

15 Old Woking to Send Church

About 8 km/5 miles with an extension of 1 km/¾ mile via Papercourt Lock; a flat walk in the Wey valley; sometimes flooded in wet seasons.
OS maps 1:25000 145 Guildford, 1:50000 186 Aldershot.

Start from Old Woking car park, TQ 018 569.

Linking walks 16✿ 17✿ 18☆ ⑩✳ **The White Hart** ☎ 01483 763202
The New Inn ☎ 01483 762736

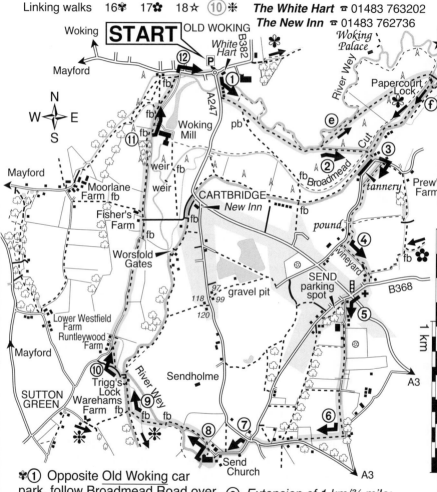

✳① Opposite Old Woking car park, follow Broadmead Road over the River Wey to the end of the houses L (150m) then diverge L on the track to the fields (100m). Don't take the R fork to the pillbox. Either join the winding river bank path L or stay on the main path skirting the meanders to the fork after the 2nd river loop (800m). ✿☆

ⓔ *Extension of 1 km/¾ mile: Fork L along the meadow and cross the Navigation (600m).*
ⓕ *Go R along the towpath and cross the next bridge L (700m).* ➜③
② Fork R towards the L end of the long building, Send Tannery, crossing the Broadmead Cut and the Wey Navigation (300m).

③ Walk along the end of the Send Tannery buildings (50m) and ahead on the lane (50m). Just before the house drive L pass R through the hedge into the field and follow the path at the R margin past a gate R (500m) and on to the end opposite a house R (150m).

④ Go L round the corner and on along the edge past the vineyard to the next corner near houses, (250m) then R to the road (100m).

⑤ Walk R to Send crossroads (150m) and ahead (50m). Turn L up Bush Lane to the school (150m). At the school gate turn L outside the fence and keep on at the edge of the field (400m) then on a tarmac track (60m). At the bend continue ahead through the field initially beside a hedge then over to the trees with houses behind (250m).

⑥ Don't join the lane L but turn R at a right angle on the right of way (often obscure) over the field. Aim for the nearest house ahead and cross into the next field 50m from the road L in the trees. Keep on towards the house and join the road from the corner of the field (300m). Go R along the road down to the junction (200m) and ahead to the staggered crossroads (60m).

⑦ Walk down the lane L and into Send churchyard (250m).

⑧ Go round the church and out at the other gate (100m). Turn L on the footpath from the drive outside the garden (50m) and keep on beside fields to cross the high footbridge over the River Wey (500m). Follow the river bank until it bends R (100m) then diverge slightly L to the visible bridge over the invisible Wey Navigation. Aim L

of the straight line to cross the low bridge over a ditch (200m). ✳

⑨ Don't cross the Navigation here but walk along the towpath R to Trigg's Lock (250m).

⑩ Cross the canal and start along the track (80m). Enter the first field R and cross diagonally to the far end of the buildings L (250m) then take the concrete track over the ditch away from Runtleywood Farm and keep on along the L edges of the fields to the drive at Fisher's Farm (800m). Enter the field ahead and carry on at the R edge (350m). Go through the thicket under power cables (100m) and on along the next field (100m).

⑪ Cross the next bridge R over the stream but go on in the same direction (70m). Just after the bend in the drive at Woking Mill (30m) re-cross the stream and follow it to the R corner of the field (300m). Exit to the drive and the main road (30m).

⑫ Walk R along the main road (see the mill through the trees R) to the road junction (250m) near the car park and **White Hart**.

Send is SANDE in the Surrey folios of the Domesday Book, a manor taxed for 20 hides, five fisheries and two mills. The present village is a network of ribbon developments along the roads but in Saxon times would have been a mile away near the church and river. The church, St Mary the Virgin, stands on a gravel bluff beside the Wey floodplain. It has a chancel dating from about 1240 still with the original lancet windows on the south side. The nave was rebuilt in the 14th century and the timber porch added late in the 15th century. Send had a church in the Domesday Book, presumably on the same site.

16 Old Woking, Newark and Cartbridge

A Wey Navigation walk. About 8 km/5 miles, flat but boggy in winter. The drier extension 4km/2½ miles and short cut of 2½ km/1½ mile may be used together. OS maps 1:25000 145 Guildford, 1:50000 186 Aldershot + 187 Dorking.

Start from Old Woking car park, TQ 018 569, or the Newark Bridges car park, TQ 039 573.

Linking walks
15❀ 17★ 18❊
21◇ ⑪ ❀

The White Hart
☎ 01483 763202
The New Inn
☎ 01483 762736
The Seven Stars
☎ 01483 225128

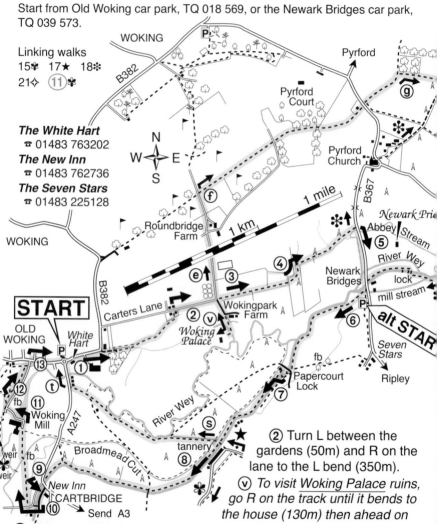

② Turn L between the gardens (50m) and R on the lane to the L bend (350m).

ⓥ *To visit Woking Palace ruins, go R on the track until it bends to the house (130m) then ahead on the path (100m) and R over the moat (100m). Return.*

ⓔ *Extension of 4 km/2¾ miles: Stay on the drive round the bend and through the S-bend at Roundbridge Farm (450m). Continue ahead up between the fields and through the golf course (250m).*

① From Old Woking car park go L on High Street to the bend (250m). Take the track ahead at the corner (100m). After the cemetery gate continue ahead under the trees (100m) and over the field beside the lesser ditch to the little bridge behind the houses (350m).

(f) *Watch out for the cross path under trees and follow it R, over a drive (600m), up beside the wood (350m) and on to the road (350m). Slightly L continue opposite on the path to the wood (300m).* ❈

(g) *Take the side path R to the bottom of the field (300m). Slightly R, go on in the same line between fields then on the road (450m).* ✧

Just into the drive of Pyrford Place (50m) take the path in the field R beside the drive (120m).

(h) *In the next field cross diagonally to the gate R (100m). Exit and keep on ahead beside the ditch (100m), then on the other side, to the end of the wood (200m). Go over the golf course slightly L to the footbridge (100m) and on to the end of the channel (100m). Turn L to the trees at the edge (150m) and go out to the Navigation then R (200m). Cross at* Walsham Gates *(100m).* ★

(i) *Follow the towpath R, crossing at the next lock (900m).The ruin R is Newark Abbey. Keep on to the road at Newark Mill (300m).* ➔**(6)**

(3) At the bend take the footpath ahead twixt fence & ditch (350m) and through the next field (150m).

(4) Cross the ditch at the end (before a pylon) and turn L. Follow the ditch round the bend L into the next field (120m) then turn R to the next pylon (150m) and keep on, L of the ditch, to join the road at the bridge (300m). ❈

(5) Cross to the pavement. Follow the road R over the Abbey Stream (Newark Abbey ruins far L) then the River Wey (200m) then the Wey Navigation (100m). ★

(6) Opposite Newark Mill house take the path to the meadows. Cross the mill leat (100m) and carry on along the river bank to Papercourt Lock (700m).

(7) Cross the bridge and continue on the other side to the next footbridge (700m). ❈

(s) *Short cut, saving 2km/1¼ mile: Turn R on the footpath over the meadows to the river (300m) and keep on (L) to the road (900m). Turn R to High Street (150m).*

(8) Go on along the towpath opposite Send Tannery. Disregard the next footbridge (700m) and keep on to Cartbridge (800m).

(9) After the road bridge ascend to the road and cross the water towards the ***New Inn*** (100m).

(10) Walk along the track between the pub and the Navigation (150m) then cross the footbridge R, and a drive, to the cart track (50m). Go L on the track briefly (50m). After the cart bridge take the path R through the meadow R to the footbridge over Broadmead Cut (300m). Keep on to the R edge of the large building, Woking Mill (250m).

(11) Join the drive ahead (40m) and go L round the building (150m).

(12) Don't follow the next bend in the drive but go on through the trees and over the footbridge (50m) then follow the ditch R and exit to the bridge at the end (350m).

(13) Walk along High Street R to the road junction (250m) near the ***White Hart*** and car park.

17 Newark Priory, Ripley and Papercourt Lock

About 7 km/4¾ miles with an extension of 1½ km/1 mile; a flat Wey Navigation walk with many possible variations; few stiles; OS maps 1:25000 145 Guildford, 1:50000 186 Aldershot + 187 Dorking.

Start at Newark Bridges car park, TQ 039 573, 100m S of the bridge with traffic lights, or at Ripley Green car park, TQ 053 571, off Ripley High Street.

Linking walks 15 ✿ 16 ★ 18 ✳ 21 ☆ 22 ✪ ⑪ ✿

The Half Moon ☎ 01483 224380
The Talbot ☎ 01483 225188
The Anchor ☎ 01483 211721
The Seven Stars ☎ 01483 225128

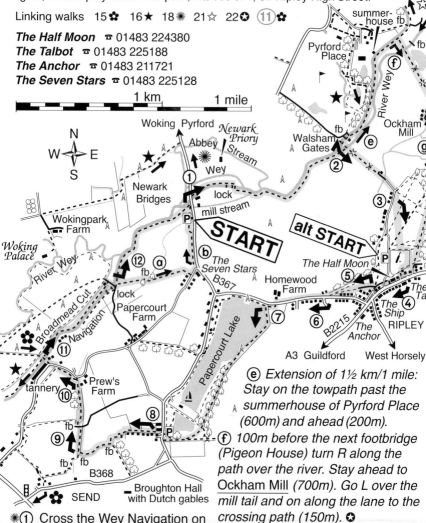

✳① Cross the Wey Navigation on the road bridge and turn off on the towpath R. Follow it past the ruins of Newark Priory far L (400m), over Newark Lock and on to the lock keeper's cottage at Walsham Gates (turf lock) (900m). ✳☆

ⓔ *Extension of 1½ km/1 mile: Stay on the towpath past the summerhouse of Pyrford Place (600m) and ahead (200m).*

ⓕ *100m before the next footbridge (Pigeon House) turn R along the path over the river. Stay ahead to Ockham Mill (700m). Go L over the mill tail and on along the lane to the crossing path (150m). ✪*

ⓖ *Turn R. The bridleway crosses a bridge (50m) and winds to a second bridge (300m). Over this bridge turn L (8m) then R. Stay ahead under the trees in a straight line to the main road in Ripley (600m). ➤④*

② After seeing the lock, return over the sluice gates and take the footpath straight on between the fields, then the track ahead past a house to the road at the edge of Ripley Green (600m).

③ Diverge from the road over the grass making for the distant row of buildings. Skirt the cricket field to the clubhouse with clock and pass between the buildings to the main road opposite the **Talbot** (600m).

④ Turn R along Ripley High Street past the **Half Moon** and side lane (200m). (The **Anchor** and church are further on.)

⑤ Opposite the **Ship** turn R between the buildings to the Green (50m) then L on one of the paths to the narrow extremity of the Green and the road (300m).

⑥ Follow Newark Lane out of the village past Dunsborough House's twin lodges to a field L (400m).

⑦ At the end of the field go L through the hedge to the gravel pit lake and L along the water's edge (350m). After the pylon (100m) fork L into the wood. Keep on (500m) and eventually curve R up beside a field to the road (300m).

⑧ Cross the lane slightly R (50m). Enter the gateway R of the houses and follow the path behind the houses to the field (150m). Keep on along the winding L edge to the end of the field and out to the T-junction (450m). ✿

⑨ Turn R between the hedge and the stream (200m) then cross the bridge and follow the stream R almost to the lane (350m).

⑩ Go L beside the lane (150m) then join the lane to the bend at Send Tannery (30m). Walk down the footpath at the R end of the building and over the Navigation footbridge (50m). ★

⑪ Follow the towpath R (700m). Across the meadows L see Old Woking church and part of Woking Palace - an isolated grey building.

⑫ At Papercourt Lock re-cross the Navigation. Either turn L and carry on along the bank to Newark Bridges (800m) or

ⓐ *Go straight over the field to the footbridge (200m) and on in the same line, then between houses to the **Seven Stars** (300m).*

ⓑ *Turn L to return to Newark Bridges, along the R verge then the footpath under the trees L.*

Tufted Duck

Ripley was part of Domesday Book Send. High Street was the old London to Portsmouth road hence the nautical pub names. *The Talbot* with Georgian façade was the post house and looks much as it would have in stage-coach days. The Green is said to be the largest in England; cricket has been played on it since about 1700, the club dating from 1743. The church, St Mary Magdelene, was rebuilt in 1846 with the Norman chancel. A round window in the south aisle commemorates Herbert Liddell Cortis the first man to cycle 20 miles in an hour. The lodges in Newark Lane are 1939 Tudoresque.

Papercourt Farm gave its name to the lock and the gravel pit lake. The earliest form is *Pappeworth* in 1204 meaning Pappa's Farm. *Court* was probably added as an embellishment.

18 Newark Mill to Pyrford Lock

About 8 km/5 miles with two shorts cuts each of about 1 km and an extra loop of 1½ km/1 mile; across water meadows and fields and along the Wey Navigation; almost level.
OS map 1:25000 145 Guildford, 1:50000 186 + 187.

Start at Newark Bridges car park, TQ 039 573.

Linking walks 15✴ 16✳ 17✺ 19✿
19✿ 21✳ 22✪ ⑪✿

The Seven Stars ☎ 01483 225128
The Anchor ☎ 01932 342507

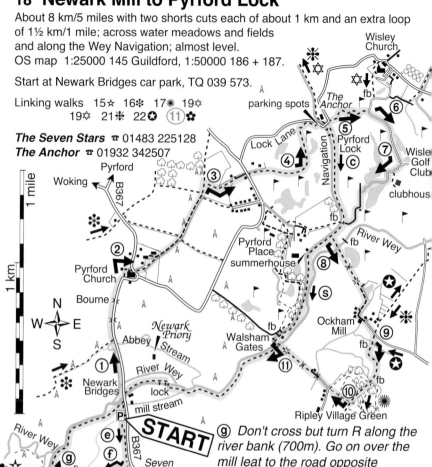

© Crown Copyright
MC 100011861

✳✿✴ⓔ *Extra loop of 1½ km/1 mile at the start or end: Follow the path beside the car park S (300m).*

ⓕ *Turn into the side lane next to the **Seven Stars** (100m) then R along the passage beside the first house (70m). In the field aim diagonally L for the footbridge (in trees) then in the same line for the bridge at Papercourt Lock (500m).*

ⓖ *Don't cross but turn R along the river bank (700m). Go on over the mill leat to the road opposite Newark Mill house (800m).*

① Cross the Wey Navigation road bridge to the pavement and go on beside the road over the River Wey and the Abbey Stream. The ruin far R is Newark Priory. Keep on along the pavement (800m).

② At the bend climb the valley side footpath ahead to Pyrford Church (60m) then cross the road and go up through the graveyard (100m). Pass through the next field to the far corner (100m). Join the track outside and go R along the field boundaries (550m).

36

③ Carry on ahead into the last field below the wood (70m) but, in mid-field, just before the pylons turn R across to the edge (100m). Go round the protruding corner, on along the L edge and out via the drive to the road at Glebe House (200m). Opposite, take the path beside the drive (200m). At the golf course keep on ahead with the waymarks (300m).

④ The signs then go L along a track (200m). Just before the road turn R around the perimeter of the golf course to the bridge near Pyrford Lock and the ***Anchor*** (200m). Cross the canal. ✱☼

ⓒ *Short cut of 1 km/¾ mile: Follow the towpath past the lock and on to the next footbridge, Pigeon House Bridge (600m).* ◆⑧

⑤ Take the footpath in line with the bridge, winding to the tarmac drive on Wisley Golf Course (250m). (Wisley Church far L , can be reached via a footbridge L after the R bend in the drive).

⑥ Go R along the tarmac track towards the clubhouse (400m).

⑦ Just before the club car park, fork R and keep on along the drive winding between ponds (400m). At the track T-junction go L, winding R, L to the towpath at Pigeon House foot Bridge (600m). Turn L.

ⓢ *Short cut of 1¼ km/¾ mile past the* summerhouse of Pyrford Place*: Stay on the towpath to Walsham Gates (900m).* ◆⑪ ahead.

⑧ Keep to the towpath (120m) then take the footpath L, over the River Wey and on. At the track, continue to Ockham Mill (700m), L over the mill tail and along the lane to the cross path (150m). ✩

⑨ Turn R. The bridleway crosses a bridge (50m) and winds to a 2nd bridge (300m). ✳ Stay ahead out of the trees to a cross path on Ripley Green to houses R (200m).

⑩ Turn R across the grass to the nearest house R (200m) and go down the lane beside it over the millstream to the next house (200m). Keep on along the path between the fields (300m). Cross the sluice gate bridge and go round to the lock keeper's cottage to see Walsham Gates, a turf lock (100m). Turn back.

⑪ Cross the sluice bridge (100m) then stay on the tow path (1000m). Cross the Navigation at the lock near the Newark Priory ruin. Carry on to the road (350m). Cross Newark Bridge to the car park.

Pyrford before the 19th century was two clusters of farmhouses. That near the old church is little altered; the other has been replaced by large housing estates - part of Woking since 1933. It first appears as PYRIANFORD in a charter of King Eadwig granting land in 956. In the Domesday Book it was PELIFORDE a manor of 8 hides partly in Windsor Forest given by William the Conqueror to Westminster Abbey.

Pyrford Church, St Nicholas, is not at the centre of modern Pyrford. It is one of the oldest churches in Surrey still in original Norman form apart from some of the windows. Points of interest: wall painting fragments of about 1140 and 1200, 12th century chancel and door arches, 14th century east window, Tudor pews, pulpit of 1628.

Pyrford Place is a modern block of apartments but the summerhouse on the canal bank is the original Tudor building. John Donne lived here after being undone by marrying the 17 year old Anne More of Loseley in 1601.

19 Basingstoke Canal meets Wey Navigation

About 7½km/4½ miles with an extension of 2½ km/1½ miles via Byfleet and Wisley Churches. A flat walk along the towpaths, made circular by town roads. Best when spring flowers are in the gardens. OS maps 1:25000 145 Guildford +160 Windsor, 1:50000 176 West London + 186 Aldershot.

Start in Shearwater Road, parking in the wide section near the railway bridge, TQ 037 607, or in one of the side roads. There is parking beside the towpath at Scotland Bridge, TQ 046 615, Old Parvis Road, TQ 055 612, and Murray's Lane, Byfleet, TQ 056 604.

Linking walks 13✿ 14✿ 18✿ 20✿ 21✳

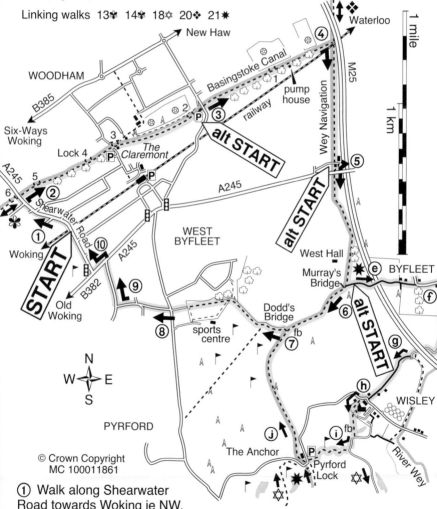

① Walk along Shearwater Road towards Woking ie NW.

② At the Basingstoke Canal go R on the towpath from Lock No 6 past Locks 5, 4, 3 & 2 to the next road at Scotland Bridge (1400m).

③ Stay on the towpath to Lock 1 (550m), the pump house (100m) and the Wey Navigation junction under the M25 (350m). ✤

④ Cross the footbridge and turn R. Follow the towpath under the (London-Southampton) railway bridge and on to the next road bridges (800m).

⑤ Ascend to the road, skirt round the works yard and carry on along the towpath to Murray's (cart) Bridge at Byfleet (850m). ✳

ⓔ *Extension of 2½ km/1½ miles: Go L on the track from the bridge, over the M25 and ahead on the road to* Byfleet *Church (750m).*

ⓕ *Enter the churchyard and follow the footpath, parallel with Sanway Road, out to the road junction (250m). From the road bend carry on along the narrow road ahead then the hard track and pass under the M25 (350m).*

ⓖ *When the hard track enters an enclosure, take the track R beside the fence to* Wisley *(400m).*

ⓗ *At the road go R briefly (50m) and enter the churchyard L. Pass round the church and follow the*

path through Wisley Golf Course, over the footbridge to the tarmac drive (300m).

ⓘ *Go R on the drive (100m) then turn off at the bend along the winding footpath to the Wey Navigation at Pyrford Lock and the* **Anchor** *(250m).*

ⓙ *Go past the pub, along the towpath, to the first footbridge over the Navigation (900m).* ➤⑦

⑥ Keep on beside the Navigation to the next footbridge (900m). ✡

⑦ Cross the Navigation and follow the boundary path ahead or the lesser path parallel with it at the edge of the golf course. After the golf course (500m) keep on through the field and out between houses to the road (400m).

⑧ Cross and follow the Holybank Road, opposite, to the end (400m).

⑨ Go R to the main road in West Byfleet (300m).

⑩ Turn L (100m) then R along Shearwater Road to the start.

SUSSEX was one of the locomotives that pulled the first regular trains to Woking in 1838. The London & South West Railway Company bought twelve similar engines @ £1,650 each from Tayleurs of Newton-le-Willows, Lancashire - presumably to be delivered by ship. With only single drive wheels and 8 tons weight they were quickly superseded. *L&SWR Locomotives 1838-53* D Bradley 1965 © Wild Swan Publications

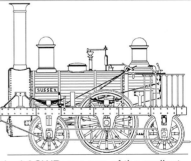

The **London - Southampton** main line of the L&SWR was one of the earliest railways to open for long distance public traffic. The first railways were private or linked only two stations but, once proved, gave rise to the notion in England and America of trunk railways with numerous stations. The L&SWR was the 4th of these, preceded only by the Baltimore & Ohio Rail Road 1830, the South Carolina Rail Road 1831 and the Grand Junction Railway (from Birmingham) 1837. The first public train to Woking Common Station ran on 21st May 1838 - a week before the first GWR train to Maidenhead. The Southampton and London halves were linked in 1839 and the London terminus moved from Nine Elms to Waterloo in 1848. Electric trains ran from Surbiton to Woking in 1936.

20 The Navigation, Coxes Lock and Wey Bridge

About 5½ km/3½ miles; along the Wey Navigation and River Wey, with non-circular extensions of 3½ km/2 miles to the River Thames and 2½ km/1½ miles to the Basingstoke Canal junction; flat, surprisingly shady and tranquil.
OS maps 1:25000 60 Windsor, 1:50000 176 West London.

Start from the car park at New Haw Lock, TQ 055 630. On the extension, start from the riverside car park in Weybridge, TQ 075 657.

Linking walks 19❖ 33★ 34❄

The White Hart ☎ 01932 842927
The Old Crown ☎ 01932 842844
The Minnow ☎ 01932 831672
Thames Court ☎ 01932 221957
Nauticalia Ferry 01932 254844

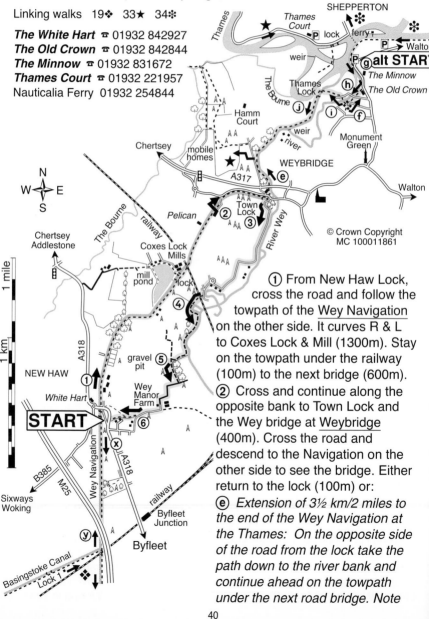

© Crown Copyright
MC 100011861

① From New Haw Lock, cross the road and follow the towpath of the <u>Wey Navigation</u> on the other side. It curves R & L to Coxes Lock & Mill (1300m). Stay on the towpath under the railway (100m) to the next bridge (600m). ② Cross and continue along the opposite bank to Town Lock and the Wey bridge at <u>Weybridge</u> (400m). Cross the road and descend to the Navigation on the other side to see the bridge. Either return to the lock (100m) or:

ⓔ Extension of 3½ km/2 miles to the end of the Wey Navigation at the Thames: On the opposite side of the road from the lock take the path down to the river bank and continue ahead on the towpath under the next road bridge. Note

for future use the little footbridge L just before the R curve (300m). ★
Stay on the towpath past the weir where river & canal split (400m) to Thames Lock *(400m). From the footbridge see the third lock gate. Keep on. Avoid a side path L. Cross a tarmac drive (150m) and the River Wey footbridge (50m).*

(f) *At the little road go L, ahead on the path between houses, over another road and on to the main road at the* **Old Crown** *(200m). Walk down the road to the River Thames (200m), through the car park and on along the river bank to the bend (150m).* ✣

If you cross the Thames, walk L to Shepperton Lock *and* **Thames Court** *then return by the same route to the old Wey bridge.*

(g) *If starting from the Thames-side car park: Follow the road away from the river past the* **Minnow** *(100m) to the* **Old Crown** *(100m).*

(h) *Turn R between the pub and its car park and follow the footpath between houses, over a road and ahead (200m).*

(i) *Just into the next little lane turn R over the River Wey footbridge and the tarmac drive (50m). Go ½L on the footpath, avoiding a side path R, to Thames Lock (150m).*

(j) *Cross the footbridge and go L along the Wey Navigation past the second weir L where it rejoins the river (400m), round the twist in the river at the house (100m), under the modern road bridge and up onto the old Wey Bridge in Weybridge (300m).* ➔(3)

(3) Go down the little road round the end of the lock (250m) and on beside the river with several bends

to the mobile home estate (850m). Take the road along the L boundary to the 4-way junction (80m).

(4) Follow the curving road L (50m) then cross the railway R. Keep on along the footpath to the next field (70m) then on the track round L to the River Wey (120m) and beside it (300m). Eventually the track bends away to a T-junction (150m).

(5) Turn L (200m). At the next T- junction turn R and follow the track round a L bend (100m) then a R bend and L to the farm house (100m). Join the tarmac drive and follow it round the R bend (50m) and on to the houses R (200m).

(6) Just before the houses take the footpath R round the end of the field and join the road near the bridge over the Navigation at New Haw Lock (250m). The **White Hart** is just over the bridge.

(x) *Extension of 2½ km/1½ miles to* the Basingstoke Canal: *From New Haw Lock follow the towpath away from the road all the way to the M25 bridge (1000m) and under it to the branching Basingstoke Canal and the* London-Southampton *railway bridge (200m).* ❖ *Return.*

(y) *Follow the towpath under the M25 to New Haw Lock (1200m).*

Coxes Lock Mill is now apartments but until 1983 made flour from grain brought by barge from London Docks. The mill had good connections by rail and road and kept up with the latest technology with water turbines, roller mills and, latterly, electric power. The first mill was built in 1776 to exploit the Wey Navigation. From 1783 to 1829 there was also an iron forging mill and from 1834 part of the flour mill was used for silk weaving. The tall building dates from 1900.

21 Wisley, Pyrford Lock and Byfleet Manor

About 8 km/5 miles; flat; a Wey Navigation walk but near the M25 and through a housing estate to make the route circular. OS maps 1:25000 145 Guildford +160 Windsor, 1:50000 187 Dorking.

Start from Wren's Nest car park, Wisley, TQ 065 589, or the roadside at Pyrford Lock, TQ 053 593, or in Murray's Lane near Byfleet old church, TQ 060 604.

Linking walks 16◇ 17☆ 18✳ 19✱ 22◆

The Anchor ☎ 01932 342507

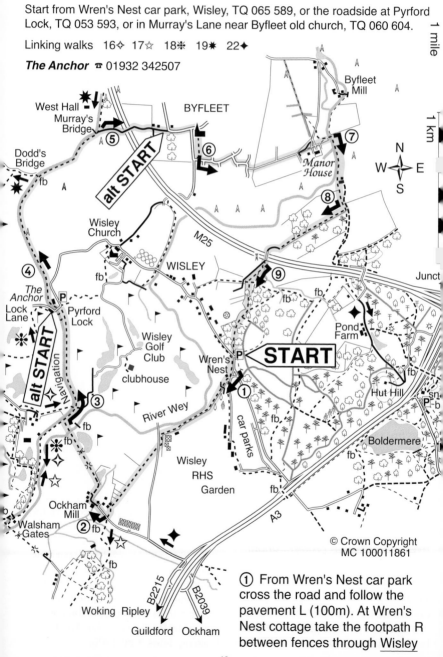

© Crown Copyright
MC 100011861

① From Wren's Nest car park cross the road and follow the pavement L (100m). At Wren's Nest cottage take the footpath R between fences through Wisley

42

Garden and beside the River Wey to the next lane (800m). Cross and continue diagonally over the fields. After the houses skirt round a garden to Mill Lane (600m). ☆

② Turn R along the lane to Ockham Mill (100m). Cross the mill tail and stay ahead on the track past the houses (200m). Continue on the footpath and cross the river to the Wey Navigation (450m). ✳◇

③ Go R on the towpath, passing Pigeon House (foot) Bridge L and a footpath from Wisley Golf Course R (100m). Carry on to Pyrford Lock and the road bridge (600m).

④ From the bridge follow the Wey Navigation towpath past the *Anchor*, a pylon (500m) and Dodd's Bridge L (400m) ✳ and keep on to pass under the next bridge (Murray's) (500m).

⑤ Join the track from this bridge and cross the motorway (250m). Keep on ahead to Byfleet Church (400m). Turn R on the path through the middle of the churchyard to the road behind (250m).

⑥ On the road go L (300m). Take the 3rd R and go round the R bend in Fullerton Road to the concrete farm track L between houses (150m). Follow it across the field to the R bend at the hedge (400m). Through the gate, stay ahead to the slight L bend (50m) then follow the path R beside a garden hedge (30m) and ahead along the wall of Byfleet Manor House (100m). At the third drive bear L to the larger path and footbridge (30m).

⑦ Cross the River Wey and turn R beside it. Pass a house near the bend in the river (300m) and carry on past the next field R (250m). ✦

⑧ At the wood enter the field R. Go down the L edge, through a belt of trees and on to the end (500m). Outside go R up the curving track over the motorway (100m).

⑨ Just after the bridge (15m) drop down the steps L. Turn R & L into Wisley Common. Follow the path near the R edge of the wood (200m), over a crosspath from the fields and ahead through the trees to Wren's Nest car park (500m).

Locks with pairs of gates are pound locks. The earliest known were on the Peking Grand Canal before 1300. By the next century they were in use in Holland. The first recorded in Britain were installed at Exeter around 1567. Experience with locks to adapt rivers as Navigations made possible the true canals. The first to be independent of a river in England was built in 1761 by the Duke of Bridgewater to convey coal from his mines to Manchester.

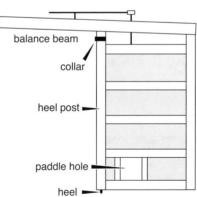

The timber gate of a small canal lock has a great *balance beam* increasing the operator's leverage but decreasing the sideways strain on the top hinge - usually a simple iron collar round the *heel post*. The iron heel at the bottom rotates in an iron socket set in the sill. The sluice for filling and emptying the lock, the *paddle gear,* is incorporated in the gate or built into the lock wall.

22 Wisley Common and Airfield

About 9½ km/6 miles with an extension of 1¼ km/¾ mile into Ockham; heath, woods and farmland. Wisley Common is boggy in winter but pools can be skirted. OS maps 1:25000 145 Guildford, 1:50000 187 Dorking

Start from the Wren's Nest car park on Wisley Lane, TQ 065 589, or from Commons Car Park off the A3/M25 slip road on Old Lane, TQ 078 586.

Linking walks 17❂ 18❂ 21✦ 23❋ 24★

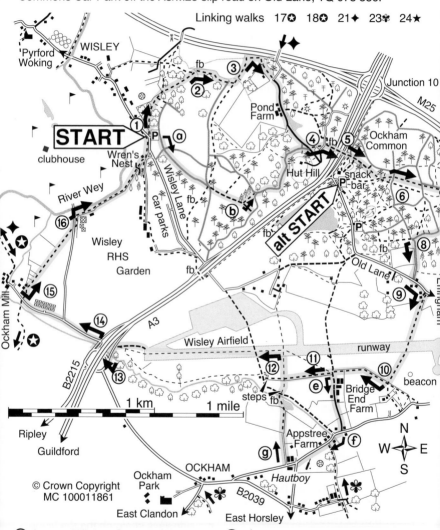

① Leave Wisley Common car park on the footpath diverging from the road northwards (away from Wren's Nest) (300m). Fork R near a field corner and keep on to the edge of the Common (250m).

② Turn R along the boundary, passing the end of a wide track, to a cross path (300m) and turn L over the bridge towards the M25 (200m).

③ Near the motorway turn R towards the hillock (100m) and skirt

R of it to the hard track (200m). Stay ahead down the track past Pond Farm R and the pond L, to Hut Hill R, watching out for the path L opposite the second exit from the track R (550m).

④ Follow the path to the tarmac drive (150m) and go straight on across the A3 footbridge (250m). (The path R skirting the hillock leads to the snack bar (200m) and Commons Car Park.)

⑤ Keep to the path ahead L of the hillock, ignoring numerous side paths, to a wide oblique cross path (300m) then fork L on the wide heath track (100m).

⑥ Use the path R of the track and stay ahead up to the Semaphore Tower (700m). ✽

⑦ Walk down through the clearing below the tower (100m) and join the downhill horse track under the trees L. Descend past side tracks L (200m) & R (150m) to the wide cross track (200m).

⑧ Go L to the road (300m).

⑨ Walk along the road L (150m). Next to a drive on the L curve, take the path R (60m). In the field continue along the hedge (100m). When it bends L go straight on, over the runway of the disused Wisley Airfield and past the circular air navigation beacon, far L, to the boundary fence (600m) .

⑩ Over the fence turn R along the path to the farm track (400m).

ⓔ *Extension of 1¼ km/¾ mile into Ockham: Go L through the farm and down to the road (400m).*

ⓕ *Walk R along the pavement (100m) then along the edge of the sports field to the side road (350m).*

ⓖ *After the barns opposite turn R up the Appstree Farm drive to the fields (250m). Continue on the path at the R edge of the field (200m) then ½L past the pond in the little valley and over the bridge and the track (150m). Go straight on up the stepped path, over the first field (100m) and ahead. →⑫*

⑪ Stay ahead at the edge of the next field to the cross path from the stile L (300m) then turn R.

⑫ Cross the field to the runway (200m) and follow it L to the end (950m). From the R corner take the track down to the road (250m).

⑬ Walk L to the roundabout, under the A3 and back on the slip road R on the other side (300m).

⑭ Turn L and stay on Mill Lane to see Ockham Mill (700m). ❂✦

⑮ Return along the lane (150m) and take the footpath, now L, up past the houses and across the fields towards the hot house of the Wisley Garden (600m).

⑯ Cross the golf club drive and turn L on the footpath briefly near the road then R. Carry on along the bank of the River Wey and between the gardens to Wren's Nest cottage (800m). Go L along the pavement to the car park opposite (100m).

ⓐ *Another time, start on the soft track beyond the car park and go R (200m). Cross a track from the road and carry on to a 6-way junction of tracks (400m). Stay ahead (300m).*

ⓑ *Take the 2nd side path L over the little rise to a junction (100m). Stay ahead on the broad winding soft track eventually passing round the foot of Hut Hill (700m). At the end cross the hard track. →④*

23 Ockham and the Semaphore Tower

About 6½ km/4 miles with an extension of
4 km/2½ miles to Ockham Church. Farmland,
bluebell wood and heath. OS maps 1:25000
145 Guildford, 1:50000 187 Dorking.

Start at Pond Car Park, TQ 079 583, off
the M25/A3 junction slip road on Old Lane.

Linking walk   22✿ 24✣

The Black Swan ☎ 01932 862364

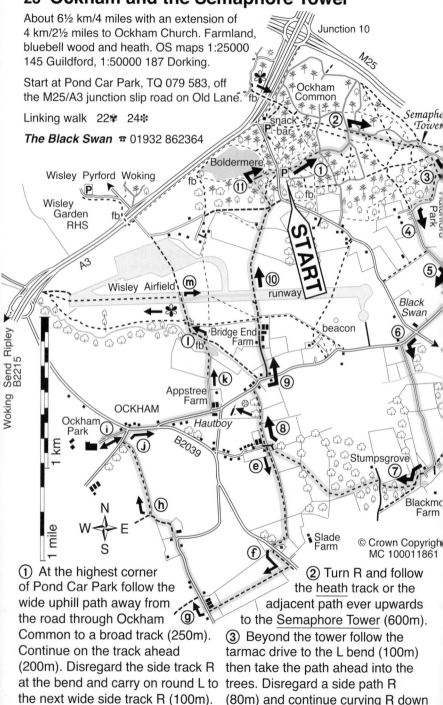

① At the highest corner
of Pond Car Park follow the
wide uphill path away from
the road through Ockham
Common to a broad track (250m).
Continue on the track ahead
(200m). Disregard the side track R
at the bend and carry on round L to
the next wide side track R (100m).

② Turn R and follow
the heath track or the
adjacent path ever upwards
to the Semaphore Tower (600m).

③ Beyond the tower follow the
tarmac drive to the L bend (100m)
then take the path ahead into the
trees. Disregard a side path R
(80m) and continue curving R down

near the edge of the wood beside Hatchford Park, round a R bend at the Samuelson monument (300m) and L down to the houses (150m).

④ Go L on the drive all the way to the road (550m).

⑤ Follow the road R round bends L & R to the **Black Swan** (550m).

⑥ After the crossroads stay on Ockham Lane briefly (100m) then turn off L on the farm drive. Follow it through the fields and round the R bend to the house (900m).

⑦ When the drive bends L stay ahead on the bridleway into the wood to the fork (70m). Bear R on the footpath to the far corner of the wood (250m). Slightly R (30m) take the path on the other side through the next wood (350m). In the field at the end, cross ½R to the middle of the bottom edge; in the next, to the far R corner. Go out to the track junction near the house (550m).

ⓔ *Extension of 4 km/2½ miles via Ockham Church: Go L along the edge of the fields until level with a house R (700m). Go R under trees R of the house to the road (100m).*

ⓕ *Cross slightly L (20m) follow the roadside bridleway (150m). Just after Slade Farm drive turn R and keep on between fields up to the next road (600m).*

ⓖ *Walk along the road R (550m). When it bends R stay ahead on the drive past the buildings then the track between fields (250m).*

ⓗ *At the L bend, take the path ahead to the next road (550m) and go R to the T-junction (100m).*

ⓘ *If you wish to see* Ockham Park *and church and quietly contemplate* Occam's Razor*, go up the drive L (200m) then return.*

ⓙ *Follow the road R to the Ockham war memorial (200m) then bear L along Ockham Lane (400m).*

Rat trap bond, a pattern of bricks laid on edge, was favoured by the Ockham estate in Victorian times, usually with elegant decorative brickwork. It can be seen in houses, barns and *The Hautboy*. Three flat bricks match two on edge in door and window reveals.

ⓚ *At the barns L just before the side road R, go up Apptree Farm drive to the fields (250m) then take the path at the R edge of the field (200m) and L of the pond in the little valley to the bridge (150m).*

ⓛ *Go L up the track to the runway in the top field (350m) or up the stepped path and over the field. ✿*

ⓜ *Walk along the runway R to the track crossing from the next farm R (500m). Turn L. ➜⑩*

⑧ Go R beside the farm. At the sports field stay outside the trees to the road in Ockham (400m).

⑨ Go R on the road (150m). Don't turn on the track L after the bridge but up the drive after Bridge End House. Continue ahead through the farm and over the field to the runway of Wisley Airfield (500m). ✿

⑩ Go on along the horse track and the house drive (600m). At the track junction don't turn to the road but carry on through the wood (150m). At the R bend, stay ahead to the boggy edge of Boldermere (100m).

⑪ Turn R. Follow the boardwalk and the rising path to the road and Pond Car Park (150m).

24 Semaphore Tower, Cobham and Downside

About 9½ km/6 miles, with an extension of 1 km/¾ mile into Cobham village and, if starting from Cobham or Downside, a short cut of 1½ km/1mile; mainly farmland; lots of stiles. OS maps 1:25000 145 + 146, 1:50000 187 Dorking.

Start from Pond Car Park, TQ 079 583 (on Old Lane off the M25/A3 slip road) or from Downside Bridge car park at Cobham, TQ 107 594, or from parking spots at TQ 107 581.

The Cricketers ☎ 01932 862105
The Plough ☎ 01932 862514

Linking walks
25★ 26❄

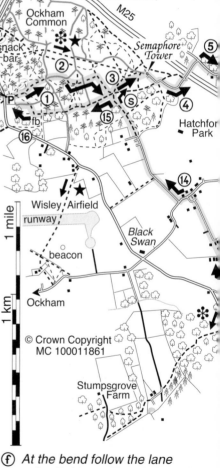

① At Pond Car Park take the main path from the highest corner to a broad cross track (250m). Stay ahead to the L bend (200m).
② Go R on the side track, round L, over another cross track (100m) and up to the next cross track (100m). Turn R to the sloping horse track (150m). Don't cross it but take the adjacent uphill path L.
③ After a short distance (50m) take the lesser side path up R to the Semaphore Tower (200m).
④ Follow the tarmac drive round an S-bend (100m). In wet periods stay on the tarmac. If dry follow the downhill horse track L. Cross the motorway to the lane (300m).
⑤ Follow the lane R to the house near the road (600m) and down to the start of the wood R (100m).
⑥ Diverge L on the footpath over the fields aiming midway between pylons (300m). Cross a footbridge near the River Mole and carry on from stile to stile to the next road (800m). Cross to the pavement.
ⓔ *Extension of 1 km/¾ mile into Cobham: Go L, over the river and round the R curve (300m).*

ⓕ *At the bend follow the lane ahead to Cobham Church (100m) and the path R though the church-yard to the next road (100m).*
ⓖ *Turn L to the main road (100m) and follow it L round the bends and over the Mole to the path from the fields R (350m).*

48

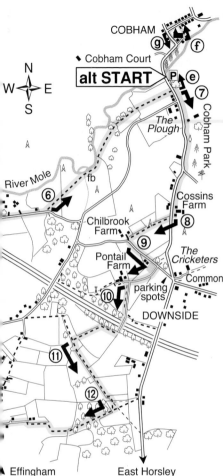

⑩ Turn L at the side drive but use the footpath R beside it (200m). Carry on over the motorway (150m) then R up the edge of the field and down beside the hedge (300m). Cross the next field ahead (60m).

⑪ Go L on the footpath along the R edge of several fields (500m).

⑫ Just into the large field with the wood ahead (40m), turn R through the trees (200m). At the next field don't follow the edge but go straight over (100m) then bear R to the nearest hedge (50m) and L along the edge (150m). Just after the houses, join the drive R and continue in the same direction to the L bend in the lane (200m) with drives branching R & ahead.

⑬ Just round the bend take the footpath R which skirts the house and garden R. Carry on between zigzag fences and across the top of a field to houses (250m). Stay ahead on the drive to the T-junction (300m) then between gardens to the road (70m).

⑭ Walk up the road L onto the rise (100m). On top take the side lane R. Continue past Hatchford, far R, to the end of the lane (600m) then on the bridleway through the trees of Ockham Common to the downhill cross track (350m).

Ⓢ *Short cut of 1½ km/1 mile if returning to Cobham or Downside: Cross the track and take the uphill path R diverging from it.* ➔③

⑮ Turn down L. Go past a side track R (200m) and smaller paths to a wide cross track before the field L (200m). Stay ahead on the footpath (250m).

⑯ After the field take one of the side paths R to the car park (200m).

⑦ Follow the road past the houses and the side road with the **Plough** (80m) then up to the side road L (450m) where Cobham Park may be seen back L. Keep on beside the main road to Cossins Farm (300m).

⑧ Just over the top of the rise cross into the first field R and follow the R edge to the lane (350m).

⑨ Walk L down the lane (350m). Just after the first houses R, turn R on the drive to Pondtail Farm. Stay on the drive round a R bend almost to the farm buildings (200m).

25 Ascot Racecourse and Great Pond

About 7½ km/4½ miles; heath and forest. Avoid on Ascot race days. A short cut of 800m/½ mile off-road may be used by Crown Land key-holders. OS maps 1:25000 160 Windsor, 1:50000 175 Reading.

Start from the kerbside in Cheapside Road, just east of Watersplash Lane, SU 939 694. No 6 Car Park (free) is near the route at the bottom end of Ascot High Street, SU 926 687.

The Duke of Edinburgh ☎ 01344 882736
The Rose & Crown ☎ 01344 882051
Lock Fyne *(Crispin)* ☎ 01344 894760

Linking walks
26◇ 27✦

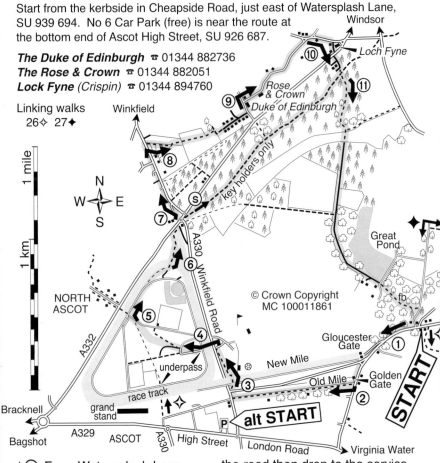

© Crown Copyright
MC 100011861

◇① From Watersplash Lane follow the pavement of Cheapside Road to the road fork (350m). See the gates to the New Mile above R then continue beside Cheapside Road to the Golden Gates (150m).

② Take the footpath L of the gates beside the Old Mile (800m).

③ At the end turn R on Winkfield Road (30m). After New Mile Road climb the steps R, cross the grass of the New Mile, continue above the road then drop to the service road under Winkfield Road (300m).

④ Go through the underpass to the inside of Ascot Race Course (100m) then diverge slightly from the road up the bank and cross the service road in the middle of the U-bend (150m). Stay ahead. Don't follow the footpath but go over the heath L of it in the same direction to the drive junction opposite the gate to Kennel Avenue (450m).

50

⑤ Don't cross the race track but turn R along the drive beside it (200m). Continue on the heath when the tarmac bends R (200m).

⑥ Halfway round the curve turn L across the race track and continue on the path to the road (300m).

Ⓢ *Short cut of 800m/½ mile for Crown Land key holders: Cross the side road R to the locked gate for the long straight track in the wood (40m). Follow the track past a side path from a gate L (800m) to the track crossing from the nearby cottages (650m). Turn R.* ✦⑪

⑦ Cross the main road L and follow the pavement of Winkfield Road L past the end of the wood R (300m) and The Avenue L (120m).

⑧ After the Avenue (150m) watch out for access to the field L, just before the end of the fields. Follow the hedge across the ends of the paddocks (200m) then enter the adjacent field L and continue in the same direction to the end of the field (50m). Exit at the middle and go on between fields (200m). At the track, turn R & L to the houses (100m). Carry on along the road to the end (200m).

⑨ Go L on the road (100m) then R after the **Duke of Edinburgh**, along the winding Woodside Road past the **Rose & Crown** (100m) to the far end (500m).

⑩ Follow the road R (150m). Before the end, cut through on the track R to the main road near the **Loch Fyne bar** *(Crispin)* (100m). Continue opposite on the track L of Woodend Cottages (100m).

⑪ Stay ahead on the forest path which eventually curves L down to a narrow field (400m). Cross the field (100m) and continue on the hard track through the trees then beside fields down round outside Great Pond (1000m). Cross the tarmac drive from the dam and follow the path down over the stream (200m) and up to another tarmac drive (100m). ✦ Walk up the drive R to the road (150m).

Ascot Race Course occupies heathland which is open to the public. Jonathan Swift wrote in a letter to Stella 10th August 1711 "We saw a place they have made for a famous horse-race tomorrow where the queen will come. We met the queen coming back ..." He missed the event but was telling of the first day's racing and of Queen Anne. She had seen the potential of Ascot Heath while following the Royal Buckhounds and commanded racing be organised next time the court was at Windsor. By the 1813 Inclosure Act, the race course was assigned to the king to be kept for racing and public use at all times. Ascot racing became fashionable in the 1780s, through the patronage of the Prince Regent who arrived in a cavalcade (then via the Golden Gate) which continues today. The New Mile replaced the original mile in 1955 so that it could be seen from the stands. Originally flat racing only, Ascot Race Course now has steeple-chasing in the winter and is a conference centre. The land is a gravel plateau, probably the 7th terrace of the river Blackwater from the Anglian glaciation, ½m years ago.   *Journal to Stella* Jonathan Swift, Ed Harold Williams OUP 1948 1169pp
Royal Ascot and its history Richard Onslow (booklet)

Ascot owes its renown to racing and its size to commuters. It grew out of hamlets in Winkfield and Windsor manors and expanded after 1856 when the branch line of the London & SW Railway opened from Staines to Wokingham.

26 Ascot Racecourse and Sunninghill Church

About 8 km/5 miles with a short cut of 1 km/¾ mile, undulating, some shade.
Avoid on race days. OS maps 1:25000 160 Windsor, 1:5000 175 Reading.

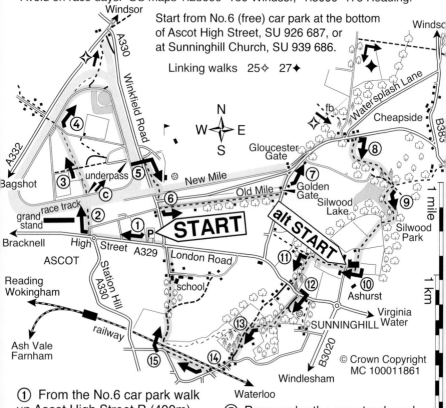

Start from No.6 (free) car park at the bottom of Ascot High Street, SU 926 687, or at Sunninghill Church, SU 939 686.

Linking walks 25✧ 27✦

① From the No.6 car park walk up Ascot High Street R (400m).

② Just after Station Hill L, turn R through the Ascot Race Course gateway. Stay ahead through the subway (R lane) to Ascot Heath within the race track circuit (250m).

ⓒ *Short cut of 1 km: Aim over the grass for the bridge R (400m).* ✦⑤

③ Continue slightly L over the grass towards the gate opposite Kennel Avenue (500m).

④ Don't cross the race track to the gate but continue on the tarmac drive beside the race track, round the N curve ✧ and back over the service road underpass (1100m). Drop down the steps R (50m).

⑤ Pass under the race track and road (100m). Climb the steps R and follow the tarmac path diverging above the road. Cross the New Mile arm of the racetrack and drop to the road (250m). Cross New Mile Road and continue to the first side path L (40m).

⑥ Follow the path beside the Old Mile (or walk along the grass) to Cheapside Road (800m).

⑦ Outside the Golden Gate follow the pavement L (150m). At the road junction see the gates above L at the end of the New Mile. Carry on ahead past the end of Watersplash Lane (350m). ✦

52

⑧ After the road junction (70m) watch out for the path back R between gardens and follow it down over the brook (feeder to Virginia Water) to the path junction outside Silwood Park (500m).

⑨ Go R on the path under trees, winding round Silwood Lake then up between fields to Sunninghill Church (700m). (Ahead beyond the church car park wall is Ashurst.) Turn R through the churchyard or the car park (100m).

⑩ Opposite the front gate of the churchyard follow the track between gardens and down into the wood (250m).

⑪ Just after the end of the field R turn L on the side path up to London Road (250m).

⑫ Follow the pavement up L (100m) and cross into the recreation ground (100m). When the track bends L stay ahead into the trees and curve R down to the track beside fields (300m).

⑬ Follow the track L past houses to the next road (300m). Walk down the road R and under the railway (Wokingham line) (150m).

⑭ Take the path R after the first house and continue to the next road (400m).

⑮ Turn R under the railway bridge and continue on the track (300m). When it bends R stay ahead up to Well Lane beside St George's School (300m) and on to Ascot High Street (200m). Cross and turn L to No 6 car park (100m).

Ashurst next to Sunninghill Churchyard is now a neo-classical block of offices. In the early years of the 20th century this was the home of the Archer-Shee family whose story provided the basis for Rattigan's play, *The Winslow Boy*.

Sunninghill is the ancient centre of the modern conurbation round about. It would have been one of the places on the edge of the lands of the people called Sunning or Sonningingas. The province of Sonning is mentioned in the charter of around 673 for its common boundary with land given by the subking of Surrey to the monastery of Chertsey. Despite its antiquity Sunninghill, is not in the Domesday Book, probably then being part of Cookham Manor. The church, St Michael & All the Angels, was re-built in brick in 1807 on its Norman site and is light and airy because of its iron piers. The Norman arch is re-used in the doorway beneath the tower. The nuns of Broomhill held it from 1200 so it has a vicar. Admiral Sir Home Riggs Popham is buried in the churchyard (near the wall on the north side). He is credited with the semaphore system between the Admiralty and Portsmouth. The 21st child of his mother, he nevertheless made headway. A contemporary of Nelson he saw action at Cape St Vincent. He sailed close to the wind politically and financially but despite years of litigation and courts martial was always at sea. He contributed to British pre-eminence in cartography by his surveys and found a new channel through the East Indies. With time on his hands, after helping put down a colonial revolt in the Cape of Good Hope, he captured Buenos Aires for the crown. He was in the commission which took the surrender of Copenhagen.

Silwood Park is an out-station of Imperial College. It is the old manor of Sunninghill and the Victorian manor house is the social centre of the college. Purchased in 1947, it enabled the college to expand out of London and houses post-graduate studies and research in nuclear physics and biology. The International Institute for Biological Control is here.

27 Windsor Great Park - South

About 9 km/5½ miles in Windsor Great Park; a tranquil route on grass or tarmac drives with an extension of ¾ km/½ mile to the Valley Garden; no stiles. OS maps: 1:25000 160 Windsor; 1:50000 175 Reading.

Start from the roadside at Blacknest Gate, SU 957 688.

Linking walks   26✦ 28☆ ⟨26⟩✳ ⟨27⟩★

The Belvedere Arms
☎ 01344 870931

© Crown Copyright MC 100011861

☆① Just inside Blacknest Gate take the path R to Virginia Water (80m) then the side path L of the lake. Stay at the water's edge until the path rejoins the road (300m).

② Cross the bridge (100m) then diverge slightly R on the sandy path across the grass. Re-join the road at the next arm of the lake (600m) and cross the dam of Johnson's Pond (100m).

54

(e) *Extension of ¾ km/½ mile into the* Valley Garden*: Take the wide path R along the curving edge of the lake to the little creek (600m).*

(f) *Cross the stream and go L up the narrow path above it (100m). After the bridge curve R (80m) and continue up the wide path to the 6-way junction on the flat top (300m).*

(g) *Don't cross the tarmac drive but turn L into the Heather Garden. Stay on the main path to the far exit (350m). Cross the drive and the grass to the Polo Club (100m).*

(h) *If polo is in progress, go L to the end of the road (200m) then R ♦(4). If not, stay ahead through the Polo Club gates and over Smith's Lawn aiming for the white Cumberland Gate and Lodge (1300m). ♦(5)*

(3) Stay on the road up the slope and past the end of the Guards' Polo Club at Smith's Lawn (900m).

(4) Diverge over the grass, L to the statue or R on the polo lawn and continue parallel with the drive to Cumberland Gate (1200m). ★

(5) Soon after the lodge bear L on the little diverging path in the trees to the road junction where the bridleway crosses (300m).

(5) Turn L on the drive towards Cumberland Lodge but almost immediately bear R on the path past the tennis court round to the next drive from the house. Walk out R to the road (400m). ✳

(6) Turn L on the side road between drives and carry on down past the Royal School and houses to the cross roads (800m).

(7) Turn L on Duke's Lane, soon passing between the fields of Norfolk Farm. Walk on the tarmac or grass beside the fence past the farm drive L (1000m), down to the bridge (500m) and halfway up to the next houses at Prince Consort's Gate (100m). ♦

(8) Turn L on the farm track in the trees after the field L and continue on the bridleway through the wood to the stone bridge over the stream L, feeding Virginia Water (750m).

(9) Turn L along the side path after the bridge (150m) and follow the arm of the lake to the road (800m).

(10) Go R to Blacknest Gate (400m).

Windsor Great Park was probably detached from Windsor Forest about 1246 when Henry III built the Great Manor as a family home adjacent to the Devil's Highway and Windle Stream (now under Virginia Water). The original Great Park reached only a little way north of the Savill Garden and was extended to Windsor Castle by Charles II when the Park was restored to the king.

Cumberland Lodge since 1947 has been the premises of the St Catherine's Foundation for students and professionals to meet and exchange ideas. The first house was built around 1650 by John Byfield, a Roundhead officer, who bought 700 acres after the Civil War. It became the Ranger's Lodge for Bab May when Charles II was restored. Under Queen Anne, the Marlboroughs were joint Rangers. George II's son, William Augustus, Duke of Cumberland, became Ranger in 1746. A major-general at 21 and victor of Culloden, he inspired Handel's Opera *Judas Maccabæus* (*See the Conquering Hero Come*) and the nick-name "Butcher Bill". The last Ranger to live here was Prince Christian of Schleswig-Holstein, husband of Helena, Queen Victoria's third daughter. In 1936, the decision to oppose Edward VIII's marriage to Mrs Simpson was taken here. *Cumberland Lodge* Helen Hudson 1997 Phillimore 236pp

28 Virginia Water, Obelisk and Smith's Lawn

About 8 km/5 miles with a short cut of 1½ km/1 mile through the Valley Garden; no mud or stiles; good for picnics; could include a visit to the Savill Garden. OS maps 1:25000 160 Windsor, 1:50000 175 Reading or 176 West London.

Start from the roadside at Blacknest Gate, SU 957 688, or from the *Wheatsheaf* on the A30, SU 981 688, or from the Savill Garden, SU 977 706.

The Belvedere Arms ☎ 01344 870931
The Wheatsheaf ☎ 01344 842057
Savill Garden ☎ 01784 485400
Garden Restaurant
☎ 01784 485402

Linking walks 27☆ ⟨27⟩☀

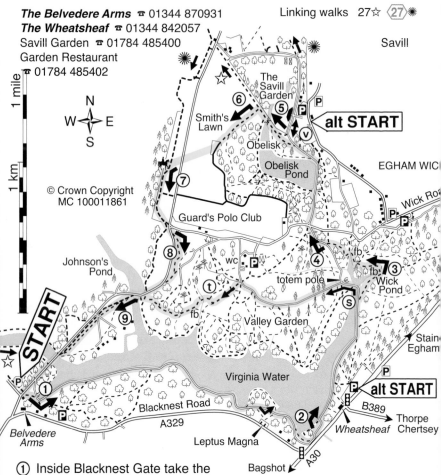

① Inside Blacknest Gate take the path R to Virginia Water (100m) and follow the tamac path around the R edge (1800m). On the grass after the bay, bear R to the ruins of Leptis Magna then rejoin the path (200m). Carry on to the corner of the lake (200m) and take the gravel path along the water's edge and down beside the cascade (150m).

② Cross the stream and keep on up to the lake. Stay at the edge, past the **Wheatsheaf** R (300m) to the end of the lake (800m).

ⓢ *Short cut of 1½ km/1 mile through the Valley Garden: Curve L between the lake and Wick Pond (100m) and take the uphill side path opposite the Totem Pole. Keep on*

56

up to the multiple path junction near the car park & house R (700m).

⓪ *Turn L on the gravel path down over the brow of the hill. Stay on this path as it winds and undulates eventually down to the road near the lake (800m).* ➔⑨

③ Branch R on the gravel footpath before the tarmac bends L round the end. Continue R of Wick Pond and cross the footbridge L (250m). Stay ahead on the winding path over another foobridge (300m) and up to the tarmac drive (100m).

④ Turn R up to the road (150m). Carry on opposite, down to and along the dam of the Obelisk Pond (400m) and up round to the side path L at the fence corner of the Savill Garden (200m).

Ⓥ If visiting the Savill Garden or restaurant stay on the drive (150m) then return.

⑤ Take the side path L above the pond and Obelisk beside the fence to the stone bridge (300m). ☆❋

⑥ Soon after the bridge (40m) bear L on the path skirting round the wood (500m). When the track bends L, keep on in the same direction diagonally over Smith's Lawn to the equestrian Prince Consort statue which is sometimes dark against the trees (300m).

⑦ Bear L along the grass near the horse track until close to the road junction (400m).

⑧ Join the road and start down the hill (50m). At the first side path L, diverge above the road to the tarmac path (250m) then descend back to the road (100m) and follow it down to the lake (100m).

⑨ Follow the road across the dam between Johnson's Pond and the lake (100m). (The Great Manor was north of the lake here.) After the dam, diverge L on the grass, across the curve in the road to the bridge (600m). Cross the bridge and follow the road or paths in the trees L to Blacknest Gate (400m).

Virginia Water was created around 1746 by William Augustus, the Duke of Cumberland (Butcher Bill), 1721-1765, when he was Ranger of the Park. He kept his troops, the 23rd Regiment of Foot, in employment to landscape the Park and dammed and dug Virginia Water, the Obelisk Pond and Great Meadow Pond. The Obelisk was erected in honour of the Duke by his father George II, though it was William IV who had the inscription added. The bridge to Blacknest Gate was re-built in 1867. Virginia Water is also the name of the adjacent commuter belt "garden town" which is part of Runnymede Borough.

The **Savill Garden** has an entry charge. It was started in 1932 by Eric Savill, the Deputy Ranger when the Duke of York (later George VI) was Ranger.

The **Valley Garden** was created by landscaping old gravel workings and is planted with acid soil plants such as heathers and rhododendrons.

Smith's Lawn is now a venue for polo matches. Smith was the riding master of the young Duke of Cumberland. During the Great War it was a Canadian Forestry Corps camp for making military huts. Edward VIII had an airstrip here. In the Second World War II it became an airfield for heavy aircraft.

Leptis Magna is a Roman town near Tripoli in Libya. The stones of the Greek-style temple were imported in 1818 and re-erected in 1827 for George IV. The ruins extend on the other side of the road in the grounds of Fort Belvedere.

29 The Thames, Ankerwyke and Wraysbury

About 7 km/4½ miles; a level route on the Thames floodplain meadows and between gravel pit lakes. Ankerwycke is known for its snowdrops in early February. OS maps 1:25000 60 Windsor, 1:50000 176 West London.

Park in the little service road off the B376 Wraysbury Road roundabout near the M25, TQ 016 726, or in the village car park at Wraysbury, TQ 005 742.

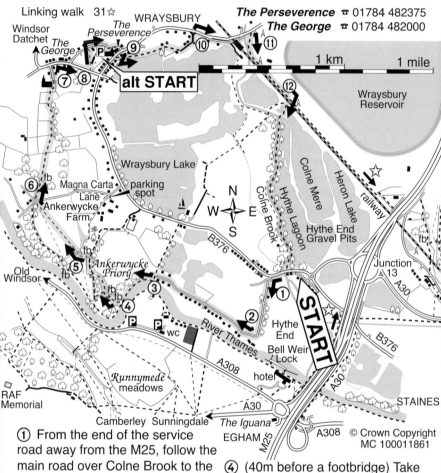

① From the end of the service road away from the M25, follow the main road over Colne Brook to the junction (150m). Turn L along Hythe End Road (400m).

② Pass round the bend by the extraction waterworks and go on to the end of the lane (800m).

③ Go through the gateway to the path. Follow it L (30m), round the bend and beside the Thames, over a footbridge (100m) and on (200m).

④ (40m before a footbridge) Take the next side path through the trees R. Cross the ditch into the meadow (40m). Bear R to the first exit (70m) and follow the path through trees beside the R ditch to the ruined St Mary's Priory, Ankerwycke L (200m) and yew R. Stay ahead (100m).

⑤ Just before the next bridge turn L into the meadow (20m). Far L is the RAF memorial on Cooper's Hill. Go on at the R edge and over the second farm bridge R into the large meadow (50m). Aim for the house far L next to the wood (450m).

⑥ Cross Magna Carta Lane at the junction and take the footpath at the L edge of the field opposite. Carry on in the same direction over the fields and up to Wraysbury Church (750m). Pass R of the church and continue ahead to the main road (150m).

⑦ Walk R along the pavement past the *George* and on (300m).

⑧ At the bridge drop to the cricket green L and pass the pavilion to the next road (150m). Turn R to the end of the road (100m). Opposite the car park exit nearest the windmill follow the path over the water (40m) and go up the lane R to the *Perseverence* (70m).

⑨ Turn R along the road (50m) and, opposite the church, take the footpath L between gardens and Wraysbury Lake (450m). Eventually join a drive from houses and continue to the road (150m).

⑩ Walk beside the road R (100m) and diverge R to the station(150m). Cross the railway footbridge and carry on over the river (100m).

⑪ After the bridge take the path R (150m) beside the Colne Brook and carry on beside the railway with Wraysbury Reservoir L (400m). ☆

⑫ Cross the railway at the first crossing point and follow the path ½L away from the railway. Continue between brook and lake to the road (1200m). Go L to the parking place.

Wraysbury was WIRECESBERIE in the Buckingham folios of the Domesday Book. The name may derive from a Saxon owner, called Wærheard or Weradus. *The George* is recorded in 1731 as the venue for the staking day meeting. The parish was enclosed in 1799; the railway arrived in 1848. The farmland which supported a population of 616 in the 1801 census mostly became 20th century reservoirs. The church, St Andrews has a 13th century chancel, nave & N aisle but was much restored in 1862 when the tower was added. The windmilll was built as a hobby project by a local resident in 1995 based on the Lacy Green smock mill of 1650 near Princes Risborough.

Wraysbury Lake and numerous other lakes in the vicinity are flooded gravel pits. The flint gravel is outwash from the Chalk of the North Downs and Chilterns of the last glaciation of the Ice Age (Devensian 50,000-10,000 year ago). The river is now higher because it has raised itself on alluvium.

Wraysbury Reservoir is 5½ km/3½ miles in circumference and 183 ha/452 acres in area. It was constructed in 1970 for the London area.

Ankerwycke was a Benedictine nunnery founded by Gilbert de Muntficher in the reign of Henry I and dissolved with the monasteries. The splendid old yew is said to be a place of tryst between Henry VIII and Ann Boleyn.

Cooper's Hill is the last hill before London and famous for its views, an outlier of Bagshot Sands and the ancient valley side of the Thames. John le Coupere appears in the local subsidy rolls of 1332 and Cowpers were frequent offenders against Forest Law in the 16th century. Englefield Green is part of Egham; it was a tithing of the parish. The name *Hingefelda* in a 967 charter lacks an *L*, suggesting the origin *Inga's clearing* rather than field of battle won by the English or land owned by an Angle.

30 Cooper's Hill, Runnymede and the Thames

About 7¼ km/5½ miles; past the JFK, Magna Carta and RAF memorials; beside the River Thames and over meadows. The meadows are occasionally flooded. OS maps 1:25000 160 Windsor, 1:50000 176 West London.

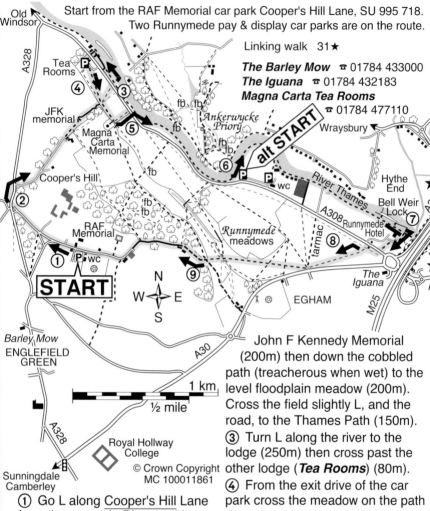

Start from the RAF Memorial car park Cooper's Hill Lane, SU 995 718. Two Runnymede pay & display car parks are on the route.

Linking walk 31★

The Barley Mow ☎ 01784 433000
The Iguana ☎ 01784 432183
Magna Carta Tea Rooms
☎ 01784 477110

© Crown Copyright
MC 100011861

John F Kennedy Memorial (200m) then down the cobbled path (treacherous when wet) to the level floodplain meadow (200m). Cross the field slightly L, and the road, to the Thames Path (150m).

③ Turn L along the river to the lodge (250m) then cross past the other lodge (*Tea Rooms*) (80m).

④ From the exit drive of the car park cross the meadow on the path diverging from the road (250m). Continue across the path from the JFK Memorial and past the Bicentennial Memorial (50m) to the Magna Carta Memorial R (100m)

⑤ Take the path over the meadow to the road and cross to the Thames (150m). Turn R and follow the river to the L bend (700m).

① Go L along Cooper's Hill Lane from the car park. Disregard L turns and continue ahead, eventually dropping to the main road (500m).

② Cross and follow the pavement down the road (Priest Hill) to the first tarmac drive R (150m). Go down the drive down through the wood and between fields (500m). Stay ahead down the path to the

⑥ Carry on along the river bank round L & R bends (500m) and on to the boatyard (350m). Keep on to Bell Weir Lock (500m) then halfway to Runnymede Bridge (100m). ★

⑦ Turn R on the paved path round the end of the Runnymede Hotel. Bear R through the parking area until you see the paved path ahead over the grass and follow it up to the road (150m).

⑧ Cross to the twin kiosk on the meadow (100m) and take the path away from the road converging on the A30 to where cross paths join it (450m). Stay ahead, bearing slightly R to pass the corner of the R hedge (300m). Continue in a straight line past another corner and on to the hedge at the foot of the slope (300m). (If boggy cross to the L hedge and follow it round.) Go up the slope still in the same direction and out to the track in the trees (100m).

⑨ Follow the winding track up Cooper's Hill (550m) then the lane (150m). After visiting the RAF Memorial (200m) continue on the road to the car park (200m).

Runnymede is Runingmeð, Ronimeð and Runimed in three surviving copies of the 1215 "Magna Carta". In Middle English *runinge* meant taking counsel and *mæd* was meadow so the site had been used for meetings before Magna Carta. Where the signing took place is unknown. The 188 acres of meadow were bought from the Crown in 1931 by Lady Fairhaven as a gift to the nation, vested in the National Trust, and as a monument to her son who died in 1929. The lodges and kiosks at the ends of the meadows were designed by Lutyens.

Magna Carta received this name, Great Charter, only when it was enlarged in a later reign. When signed and sealed in 1215 it was *Articles of the Barons*. Its historic significance is its insistence that the king could not take prisoners and taxes without just cause. In other words he had to abide by the rule of law. The text was probably self serving for the barons but it may be that the mediator, Stephen Langton, Archbishop of Canterbury, had a hand in phrasing it so it became universal. It had other provisions, eg dismissal of the king's French advisers, reversal of afforestation. *Encyclopædia Britannica* has the text.

The **Magna Carta Monument** takes the form of a miniature Greek temple with eight columns. The central plinth bears the inscription: Dedicated in 1957 by the American Bar Association, as a tribute to the Magna Carta; symbol of freedom under law. The architect was Sir Edward Maufe.

The **John F Kennedy Memorial**, designed by G A Jellicoe, is a Portland Stone block on a granite plinth, bearing the inscription: This acre of English Ground was given to the United States of America by the people of Britain in memory of John F Kennedy, President of the United States of America, 1961-1963.

The RAF Memorial (closed 4pm in winter, 6pm in summer) is for the airmen of many nations who died serving with the RAF in World War II and who have no known graves. It is a light airy building with a sombre list of 20,401 names on its walls. The architect was Sir Edward Maufe and it was opened in 1953.

Runnymede Bridge opened in 1961 for the A30 Staines bypass. In the 1970s when the M25 was added, archæologists found late Bronze Age habitation (8th century BC) at the SW end. Piles of a 50m wharf suggest the river was at the present level and already in use for trade. Bones of cow, sheep, goat, pig, wild boar and red deer were found and and bronze artifacts of continental origin.

31 **Staines Moor, Thames and Runnymede Bridge**

About 6 km/4miles with an extension of 1½ km/1 mile. Parts of the route are flooded after heavy rain. OS maps 1:25000 161 Windsor, 1:50000 176 W London.

Start in Staines from the kerbside on the B376, Wraysbury Road, near the M25 flyover, TQ 023 723.　　　　Linking walks　29☆　30★

The Bells ☎ 01784 454240　*The Swan* ☎ 01784 452494

© Crown Copyright MC 100011861

① Walk up the drive beside the motorway embankment (40m) and take the hard path R parallel with the reservoir link channel (500m).

② After the last field L drop down steps R to the path underneath. Go under the A30 and over the field to the far end of the row of houses (250m). Join the road (50m) and turn L. After the Wraysbury River R watch out for a path R (150m) and follow it over the railway (50m).

③ After the railway (100m) turn R over the river footbridge and pass under the (disused) railway bridge to Staines Moor (150m). Continue ahead to the River Colne (250m).

④ Turn L. Follow the river bank (400m) then the path near the stream to the footbridge R (100m).

⑤ Cross the stream. Go on over another stream (80m) and round R over the river footbridge (70m).

ⓔ *Extension of 1½ km/1 mile: Turn L along the river bank (200m). Cross another stream and go on between fields to join the hard path below George VI Reservoir (500m).*

ⓕ *Turn R and follow the path to the end of the reservoir (1500m) then ½R to the A30 (100m).*

ⓖ *Pass under the A30 then climb L to the road and cross the bridge (100m). Descend L to the cross path (200m). Stay ahead.* ➔⑦

⑥ From the footbridge stay ahead to a curve of the river R (300m). Continue to the next footbridge, either straight ahead or along the river bank path (400m). Cross the river and bear L. Stay with the river (150m) then pass under the A30 to the path junction (150m). Turn R.

⑦ Go up the track beside the road, round the bend, over the railway and link channel and down to the road (300m). Take the path opposite to the next road (70m).

⑧ Follow the road L to the main road in Staines (300m). Cross and carry on past the church to the **Bells** (100m) then turn R to the Thames at Church Island (100m).

If you wish to see the London Stone turn R to the park and follow the river bank (150m), then return.

⑨ Go L along the riverside path; pass under Staines Bridge (350m).

ⓘ *If you wish to see a bit of the town, carry on along the bank, over the River Colne to the Memorial Gardens (200m) then turn L past Old Town Hall (100m) and follow the road back to the river (200m).*

⑩ Cross the Thames (L of road) and drop down steps to the tow path (100m). (The **Swan** is 100m R.) Go L under the bridge and on along the river over a long footbridge (250m) to the Coal Tax post L at the retail car park (200m). Stay ahead under Runnymede Bridge (850m) to Bell Weir Lock (200m). ★

⑪ Return halfway to the bridge (100m). Take the unpaved side path R through the trees to the A30 (150m). Turn L. Follow the path beside the A30 over the Thames and down to Wraysbury Road (700m). ☆ Pass under the motorway to the starting point (200m).

The **London Stone** was set up in 1285 to mark the limit of the City of London's jurisdiction on the Thames. The original is in Staines museum; a replica on the river bank. Its position may have been at the bridge, the Middlesex boundary or the weir, then the highest tidal point. Richard I sold control of the river to the City for £20,000 in 1197 wanting money for the Crusade. The river came under the Thames Conservancy in 1857 (now the Environment Agency). In 1908 the Port of London Authority took over the tidal part below Teddington Lock.

Staines had Roman soldiers soon after the conquest - shown by pottery finds. The Roman name *PONTES* is deduced from *PONTIBUS* (at the bridges) listed at the correct distance in Iter VII of the Antonine itineraries, on the Roman road from London to Silchester (Devils Highway). Twentieth century building brought to light evidence of Roman buildings along High Street probably aligned with island-hopping bridges over the river. The Domesday Book manor of STANES was taxed for 6 mills and a weir. Saxon names like this usually derive from *stones;* a 12th century boundary mark was the Negen (nine) Stones, said to be the site of the church. The arrival of the Windsor railway line in 1848 brought Staines into the orbit of London and by 1901 the population had reached 6000. It became large enough to sustain its own industry, including the first linoleum factory, several breweries and engineering works. Noteworthy buildings are the italianate townhall, 1871-80; the *Blue Anchor* in High Street of around 1700; Dumcroft, 1631, the church, St Mary, rebuilt 1829 in Gothic revival style.

32 Thorpe Green and St Ann's Hill

About 7 km/4¼ miles with an extension of 2 km/1¼ miles to Thorpe village; fields and woods with quite a lot of road walking; undulating; brambles and nettles in summer. OS maps 1:25000 160 Windsor; 1:50000 176 West London.

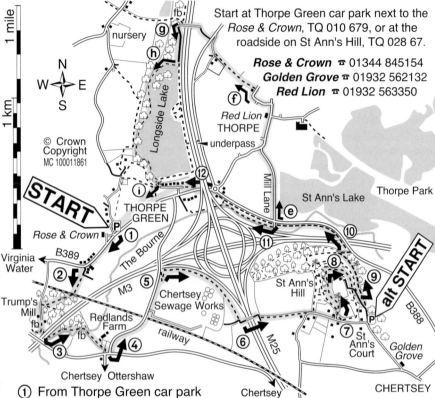

Start at Thorpe Green car park next to the *Rose & Crown*, TQ 010 679, or at the roadside on St Ann's Hill, TQ 028 67.

Rose & Crown ☎ 01344 845154
Golden Grove ☎ 01932 562132
Red Lion ☎ 01932 563350

© Crown Copyright MC 100011861

① From Thorpe Green car park cross to the **Rose & Crown** and go on along the road (300m).

② On the R bend, after the last house, go L on the track to the field (40m) and down the R edge (150m). Cross the railway lines and bear R along the path through the wood (150m) then R to the tarmac drive (50m). Walk down the drive (L) past Trump's Mill R and cottage L (100m) and on along the footpath (50m).

③ Don't cross the Bourne bridge but drop L and cross the mill tail. Stay beside the Bourne under the road (400m). At the end of the wood cross the footbridge and go up the R edge of the field past Redlands Farm, across a narrow field and R to the road (150m).

④ Turn L and L again and walk up Lyne Lane over the railway and on to the motorway bridge (700m).

⑤ Just before the bridge take the path R down the embankment and follow the edge of the road up beside Chertsey Sewage Works to the farm bridge (750m).

⑥ Cross the M25 (150m). Slightly R take the path between fields (300m). Stay ahead up the lane to the path L after The Lodge (200m).

⑦ Turn L for St Ann's Hill. Inside go L to the fence near The Lodge (70m) and ascend beside it. When the fence bends L (30m) continue up, disregarding all side paths, to the beacon on top (300m).

⑧ Just before the beacon turn R on the path which curves around the brow of the hill (200m). When the track crosses from the garden, turn L down it. Disregard the first side track L (50m) and continue to the track rising from below (100m).

⑨ Turn back L down this track (Old Coach Road) (400m).

⑩ Near the bottom, watch out for the path R and go down it to the road (Mill House Lane) (80m). Turn L and walk along the horse ride verge over the M3 (200m) and the Bourne (250m). Carry on to Mill Lane (200m).

ⓔ *Extension of 2 km/1¼ miles to Thorpe village: Walk along Mill Lane past fields (500m) then R on the road through the village to the* **Red Lion** *(200m). Go on round L & R bends to the first field (300m).*

ⓕ *Take the footpath L to the end (400m) and go R along the lane to the road (200m). A little L (30m) join the track on the other side and go over the motorway (200m).*

ⓖ *From the bridge continue round L down the track beside the M25 to Longside Lake (250m).*

ⓗ *Turn R across the N edge of the lake (60m) then follow the path round the W bank with a ditch R most of the way (750m).*

ⓘ *At the S end cross the wide footbridge near houses to the green in Thorpe Green. Bear R over the grass to the gap in the hedge then straight to the car park (500m).*

⑪ Opposite Mill Lane turn L to the river (50m). Go R along the bank (350m) and rejoin the road (100m).

⑫ Keep on to the roundabout and under the M25 (250m). Just out the other side take the path R through the trees to the green in Thorpe Green (100m) and keep on, parallel with the road, to the car park at the end (500m). The tower visible far R was part of Holloway Sanatorium.

Holloway Sanatorium was opened in 1885 for mentally afflicted women but is now apartments. Thomas Holloway, 1800-83, made his fortune from quack medicine. Pioneer of mass advertising, he spent £45,000 in 1882 all over the world. He moved to Sunninghill when he became rich - his grave is at the church. Having built the sanatorium & Royal Holloway College he left £½m.

Trump's Mill dates from before 1299 when it paid 21s 4d tithes to Chertsey Abbey. Milling ceased in 1909.

Redlands Farm is a hall house of around 1490. The second storey and chimney would have been added in the next 50 years with the jettied wing.

St Ann's Hill, a Bagshot Sand outlier, is a landmark for the adjacent M25/M3 junction. It was the grounds of St Ann's Court which Charles Fox acquired by marrying his mistress, Mrs Armistead. The Prince Regent (George IV) came here to moon over Mrs Fitzherbert and fell out with Fox when he married her. The name is from a medieval chapel on the hill. The old name was *Aldbury* from the Iron Age hill fort on top.

Thorpe, known for its theme park, is one of the earliest places documented in England. It was land called Torpe, gifted to Chertsey Abbey in the charter of 673. In the Domesday Book, four centuries later, it is TORP. Þorp was a Saxon word for village (Þ = Th). The church, St Mary, has 12th century fabric but is much restored.

33 **Chertsey Bridge to Shepperton Ferry**

About 7 km/4½ miles with short extensions; flat; over meadows and along the Thames Path with a ferry crossing. The ferry operates 8-6 weekdays, 9-6 Saturdays and 10-6 Sundays; but only until 5pm on winter weekends. OS maps 1:25000 160 Windsor, 1:50000 176 West London.

Start from Mead Lane car park in Chertsey next to the marina, TQ 054 662, or the public car park TQ 071 659, next to *Thames Court* at Shepperton Lock, or the public car park near the ferry in Weybridge, TQ 075 657. At the east end of Chertsey bridge there is a minute car park and a larger one 100m further east.

Linking walks   20★   34☆   Nauticalia Ferry ☎ 01932 254844
The Old Crown ☎ 01932 842844   **The Minnow** ☎ 01932 831672
The Kingfisher ☎ 01932 579811   **Thames Court** ☎ 01932 221957

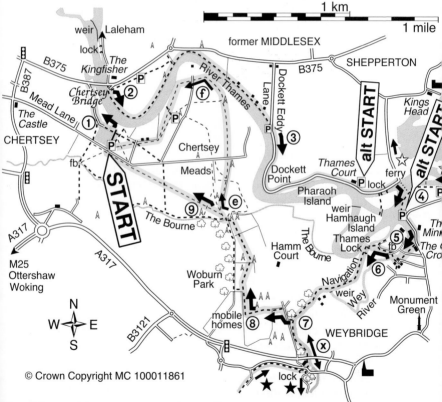

© Crown Copyright MC 100011861

① At <u>Chertsey</u> Meads car park follow the marina fence away from the road (100m) and turn L along the footpath over the marina channel (100m). Carry straight on along the road to the main road (300m) (<u>Curfew Bell</u> effigy L).

② Turn R across <u>Chertsey Bridge</u> (100m). Chertsey Lock is visible L, upstream. At the Middlesex end go round the <u>Coal Tax post</u> (with badge). Opposite the **Kingfisher** follow the Thames Path along the river bank (1600m) or the path near the road across the first meander (300m shorter).

③ At the road stay ahead on the path beside the road round Dockett Point, past the parking lot for the cars and boats for Pharoah Island residents, the **Thames Court** (1000m) and Shepperton Lock (200m). Keep to the water's edge to the Nauticalia Ferry jetty at the bend in the road (100m). ☆

④ Cross the river. From the ferry landing follow the path round the curving river bank ↘↙ to the car

---

View of the river: Facing the weir the narrow channel L is the mouth of the River Wey and the site of the wharf. The next channel is the start of the Wey Navigation and the third is the original bed of the Thames sweeping round an elongated meander from the weir opposite the *Thames Court*. Out of sight the Bourne joins the meander in the middle. The white water at the weir, used by canoeists, comes from Stoner Gut, an artificial cut detaching Hamhaugh Island within the meander. The Shepperton Lock is also artificial. Downstream of the ferry, with arching footbridge, is D'Oyly Carte Island where lived the theatrical family.

---

park (150m). Take the road ahead past the **Minnow** (200m).

⑤ Turn R between the **Old Crown** and its car park and follow the footpath between gardens, over the first road and ahead on the next path (200m).

⑥ At the little road don't continue on the next path but turn R over the River Wey footbridge and the tarmac drive (50m). Continue ½L on the footpath to Thames Lock (150m). From the footbridge see the third lockgate downstream. Go L along the Wey Navigation past

the second weir L where the river separates (400m), round the twist in the river at the house (100m) and on to the next L curve (300m). Watch out for a little footbridge over the ditch back R.

ⓧ *Extension of 600m to see the Wey Bridge: Continue on the tow path under the modern road bridge to the old Wey bridge in* Weybridge *(300m).* ★ *Go out onto this bridge then back along the tow path (300m).* ➔⑦

⑦ Cross the little footbridge to the road and go R to the gate of Hamm Court Farm (100m). Take the path L and cross the field to the mobile home estate (300m).

⑧ Go R along the edge of the field to the corner of the estate (200m) then either straight on through the fields between pylons, ultimately to the far L corner (500m) or L along the end of the estate and R down the path outside the field. Exit to the cart bridge and cross the Bourne to Chertsey Meads.

ⓔ *Extension: From the bridge go briefly L (20m) then take one of the paths directly away from the Bourne to the lane (400m). Cross and go straight on over the meads to the bank of the Thames (600m).*

ⓕ *Turn L and follow paths beside the river and round the houses to the car park at the marina (700m).*

⑨ From the bridge identify St Ann's Hill, low on the horizon ½L and aim directly for it over the meads, diverging from the Bourne; there is usually a faint path (700m). When Mead Lane converges R keep on near it to the car park near the marina (200m).

34 Walton Bridge and Shepperton

About 6½ km/4 miles but variable; along the Thames Path and on the lanes through Old Shepperton; flat. It involves a ferry crossing. The Nauticalia Ferry operates 8-6 weekdays, 9-6 Saturdays and 10-6 Sundays but only until 5pm in winter. OS maps 1:25000 160 Windsor, 1:50000 176 West London.

Start from Walton Bridge car park, TQ 092 663, or the public car park beside the *Thames Court* near Shepperton Lock, TQ 071 659, or the public car park near the ferry in Weybridge, TQ 075 657, or the recreation ground car park in Church Road, Shepperton, TQ 078 668. Linking walk 20✻ 33☆

Nauticalia Ferry ☎ 01932 254844
The Minnow ☎ 01932 831672
The Kings Head ☎ 01932 221910
The Ship ☎ 01932 227320
The Red Lion ☎ 01932 220042
The Old Crown ☎ 01932 842844
The Thames Court ☎ 01932 221957
The Anchor ☎ 01932 221

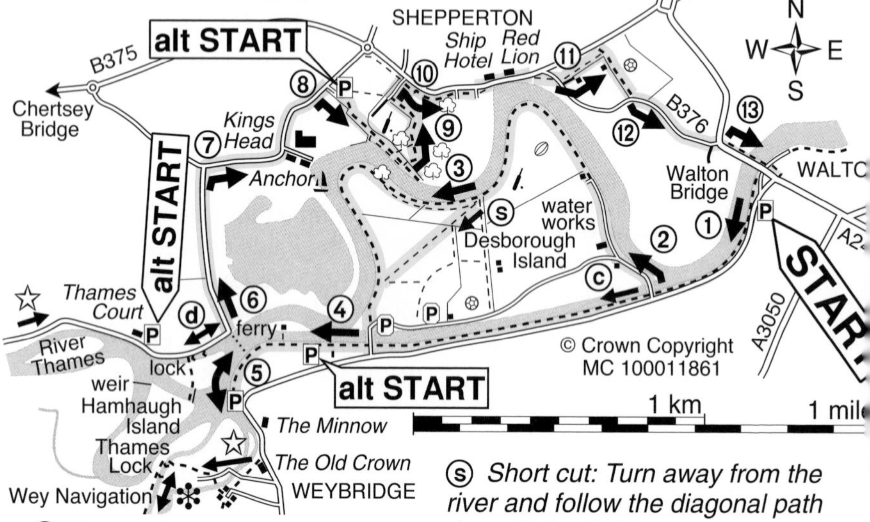

Feltham
Sunbury
N
W
E
S
SHEPPERTON
Ship Hotel
Red Lion
alt START
B375
Chertsey Bridge
Kings Head
Anchor
B376
WALTO
Walton Bridge
water works
Desborough Island
A3050
START
Thames Court
River Thames
lock
weir
Hamhaugh Island
Thames Lock
ferry
alt START
The Minnow
The Old Crown
WEYBRIDGE
Wey Navigation
© Crown Copyright MC 100011861
1 km
1 mil

① Follow the Thames Way path on the river bank upstream away from Walton Bridge, past Cowey Stakes, to the next bridge (500m).

ⓒ *Short cut of 1 km/¾ mile: Stay ahead beside the* Desborough Cut *to the next bridge (1000m).* ➧④

② Ascend to the bridge and cross to Desborough Island (200m). When the road bends L take the track beside the river to the sports field entrance (300m) then carry on along the footpath under the trees round a bend in the river until paths branch L into the fields (700m).

ⓢ *Short cut: Turn away from the river and follow the diagonal path through the fields, to the next bridge (600m). Over the bridge the route is R along the river.* ➧④

③ In the field take the path near the river (300m) then continue under the trees on the bank again opposite Shepperton Church and Manor House (600m) back to the road. Cross the bridge and drop to the river bank (100m). Turn R.

④ Continue along the Thames (upstream) past the footbridge of D'Oyly Carte Island (300m) and on round the curve. Watch out for the ferry landing (100m). ☆

⑤ Keep on round the curve in the river to the little car park (150m). ❉ (the **Minnow** and **Old Crown** are a little further along the road) then return along the river bank to the ferry and cross to Shepperton.

ⓓ *Detour: Follow the road beside the river to see* Shepperton Lock *(100m) (the **Thames Court** is 200m further on) then return to the bend in the lane at the ferry jetty.*

⑥ Follow Ferry Lane away from the river to the end (600m).

⑦ Turn R along Chertsey Road to the old Shepperton village centre (300m). After the **Kings Head** and the church carry on out of the old village (300m).

⑧ At the recreation ground car park turn R and follow the path along the edge of the field and on to the end of the wall R (200m) then join the river bank and continue (100m).

⑨ Turn L over the riverside path in the trees and go on along the winding path outside the cricket field (250m). Follow the drive towards the road (100m).

⑩ Just before the road turn R on the footpath. Follow it until it joins the road at the **Ship**. Keep on beside the road past the **Red Lion** (300m) almost to the next R, Walton Lane (100m).

⑪ Cut across the corner R and across Walton Lane and go on over the grass next to the frontages (200m). Turn R round the corner in the wall and follow the path beside the football field out to re-join Walton Lane (200m).

⑫ Turn L and follow the lane to the end (400m).

⑬ Cross the road and cross Walton Bridge (200m) and take the steps down L. Go under the bridge, back to the car park.

The **Thames** is an ancient highway for traffic. When the Runnymede M25 bridge was built, piles here found in the river suggesting a late Bronze Age wharf 50m long. A 2nd century barge exposed during building work at Barts Hospital was 15m long but there may have been larger ones as a Dutch boat of the same age was 34m long. Barges were swim-headed (punt shaped) until superseded by Newbury barges (pointed) in the 18th century. They had sails which could be deployed when the wind was in the right direction. Tow ropes were attached at the masthead. Until the 18th century towing was not done by horses but by local squads of men called *halers*.

Locks are needed because of the weirs. The weirs are needed to retain water deep enough for navigation. The earliest weirs were probably built to provide a head of water for mills so the Thames might be viewed as a series of mill ponds or pounds. The first pound locks (ie with two sets of gates) were built in the Upper Thames around 1630. They permit a weir to control the upstream level - still the main job of the lock keeper. Before that there were flashlocks, gates in weirs, that could be opened for boats to pass through (with great difficulty and hazard) and cause a flash of water to raise the level downstream.

The Port of London Authority administers the Thames below Teddington Lock. The small obelisk on the bank 250m downstream of the lock denotes the Port's limit in 1909. Above Teddington the river is now under the Environment Agency the latest successor to the Thames Conservancy of 1857 - TC on installations.

The Thames Highway Fred Thacker 1920 & 1968 David & Charles 525pp

35 Hampton Court, Ferry and Bushy Park

Read the note on the Royal Parks at the back. The route is via the Hampton Ferry which operates only in summer. About 8 km/5 miles through Bushy Park and along the Thames. The paths of Bushy Park allow many variations. OS maps 1:25000 161 London South, 1:50000 176 West London.

Start from the Diana Fountain car park in Bushy Park, TQ 160 693, or from the Hurst Park car park in East Molesey, TQ 141 692.

Linking walks 36✦ 37★

Hampton Ferry ☎ 020 8979 7471
The Bell ☎ 020 8941 8864

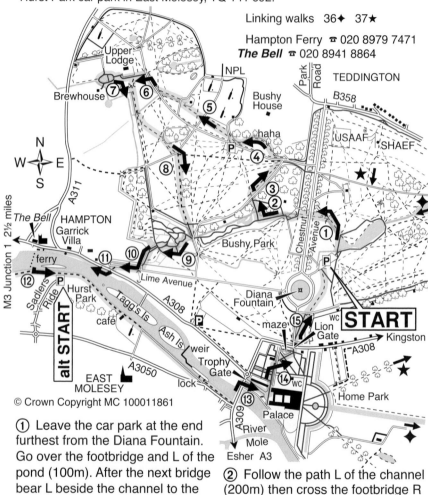

© Crown Copyright MC 100011861

① Leave the car park at the end furthest from the Diana Fountain. Go over the footbridge and L of the pond (100m). After the next bridge bear L beside the channel to the culvert-with-rail (150m). Bear L across the grass to the iron pump (50m). Stay ahead over Chestnut Avenue to the rail at the other end of the culvert (200m) then bear L to the gate in the fence (50m) and enter the Woodland Garden.

② Follow the path L of the channel (200m) then cross the footbridge R and carry on to the exit (150m).

③ Outside the fence, follow the drive R to the junction (300m).

④ Cross the road to the boundary trees and follow the path L round beside the haha of <u>Bushy House</u>, curving back near the road (350m).

70

⑤ Continue beside the trees briefly then diverge from the road across two drives towards the next house. Pass L of the garden to the drive (450m). Cross and carry on R of the water channel to the road (100m). Continue (R) on the road to the hard path L (150m). The large buildings far R are NPL.

⑥ Follow the path along the fence of Upper Lodge to the Water Garden (200m). Walk right round the ponds and back (200m).

⑦ Return until opposite Upper Lodge (100m) then take the path R along the edge of the park (250m). Over the stream join the path diverging slightly from the fence (50m) and bear L over the grass to the fenced clump of trees (250m). Pass R of the clump and continue to the tarmac drive (150m).

⑧ From the bend continue on the path parallel with, 200m from, the tree-lined R boundary (500m). Carry on between the fences of the E & W Woodland Gardens (80m). Turn R through the gate into the W garden and take the first side path L round to the oval pond (150m). Stay ahead R of it to the square pond (100m).

⑨ Near the little cascade take the hard path up on the dam L of the pond. Keep on to the garden exit (150m). Outside, turn R along the park to the end gates (200m).

⑪ Join the main road and go R along the pavement crossing as soon as convenient. Carry on, past Garrick Villa R & Temple L (400m). Opposite Hampton Church drop to the river and go along the foreshore to the ferry (100m). Cross the Thames.

⑫ Go L along the river through Hurst Park, opposite Tagg's Island and past the cricket pavilion café to the lane (900m). Stay ahead to Molesey Lock (500m) then on the path below the road to Hampton Court Bridge (300m).

⑬ Cross the river then cross the road to the Trophy Gate of Hampton Court (200m). Follow the drive to the palace forecourt (150m)

⑭ Go L through the arch to the garden and go on beside the wall to the first opening R (200m). Carry on in the adjacent garden and bear R on the diagonal path past the maze to the Lion Gate (150m). ✦★

⑮ Cross the road into Bushy Park. After the lodge bear R on the wide path to the end of the channel (250m). Cross the tarmac drive and carry on in the same direction over the grass to the car park (300m).

William IV lived at Bushy House with a mistress, Mrs Jordan, & 10 children. As the third son of George III he was not expected to become king and at 13 was put into the Royal Navy where he advanced to frigate captain. Most of his service was in the Caribbean where he became a friend of Nelson. After his life at sea he received the honorific title, Lord High Admiral, and used it to promote reforms in the RN including steam power. George IV had no heir and the second brother died, making William's kingship likely. He married a Bavarian princess, Adelaide, who ameliorated his sea dog manners. He acceeded in 1830, a year of social upheaval, and is chiefly remembered for creating 60 peers in an attempt to pass the Reform Bill. He sited no legitimate children and Queen Victoria who succeeded in 1837 was a neice.

Sailor King Tom Pocock 1991
Mrs Jordan's Profession Claire Tomalin 1995

36 Hampton Court, Kingston and Bushy Park

Read the note on the Royal Parks at the back. About 8 km/5 miles In winter the better alternative is through the formal garden of Hampton Court Palace which is free Oct - March. A detour is required when the flower show occupies Home Park. OS maps 1:25000 161 London South 1:50000 176 West London.

Start from the Diana Fountain (free) car park in Bushy Park, TQ 160 693. Public transport users might join the route at Kingston Bridge.

Linking walks 35✦ 37✲   ***Bishop out of Residence*** ☎ 020 8546 4965
White Hart ☎ 020 8977 1786

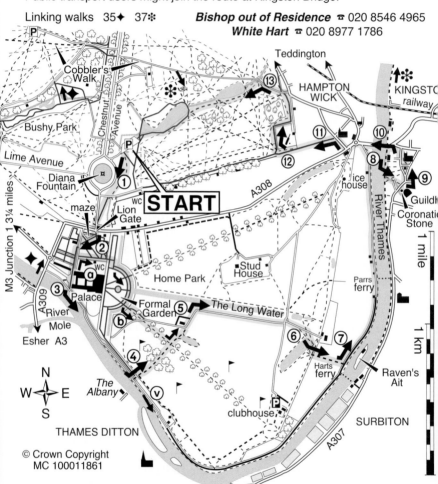

✦① From the corner of the Diana Fountain car park near the car exit, take the hard path L & immediately diverge R over the grass to the trees R of the wall (300m). Cross the drive and continue R of the water channel to the gates (250m).

② Cross the road into the Lion Gate of Hampton Court. Go along the R diagonal path past the maze (150m), and into the next garden (50m) then L along the wall, through the arch and across the forecourt to the river bank (200m).

During BST, to avoid payment at the Formal Gardens ➔③. *In winter* ➔ⓐ

ⓐ Return across the forecourt and stay ahead R of the arch (200m). Take the first path R along the edge of the garden (200m). Pass through the gate to the Formal Garden and cross to the water channel (50m).

ⓑ Turn R. Follow the channel round to the second footbridge & gate (350m). Cross into Home Park. Stay ahead in the middle of the avenue over a drive (100m) and on (300m). Turn L on the path past the pond to the drive bend at the house (150m). ➔⑤

③ Go L beside the Thames, past the palace and gardens, to the gate above steps opposite the *Albany* far R (700m).

If Hampton Court Flower Show occupies Home Park ➔ⓥ. *If not,* ➔④.

ⓥ Slightly longer variant: Stay on the river bank round the bend to Raven's Ait (2000m). ➔⑦

④ Go through two gates to Home Park. Stay ahead over the fairways, through the gap in the trees and L of the pond to the drive bend nearest the house (450m).

⑤ Continue on the drive (R of the house) to the next bend and over the grass to the Long Water (150m). Turn R and follow the bank (or the tarmac) to the crossroads (600m). Stay ahead on the drive (150m).

⑥ Diverge R on the path to the pond (150m). Go round the end then diverge L from the water to the gate (100m). Exit along the path to the Thames opposite Raven's Ait and Surbiton (250m). Turn L.

⑦ Stay beside the Thames to Kingston Bridge (1500m) and cross the river (150m).

⑧ Drop to the river bank R (S). Walk past the **Bishop** along the river (200m) then turn L beside the side stream (Hogsmill River) up to the town road (100m).

⑨ Step onto the bridge (or enter the Guildhall forecourt) to see the Coronation Stone then go L across the Market Square and along the passageway to the church (200m). Go L round or through the church to the W door and rejoin the road then R & L to the bridge (200m). ✣

⑩ From Kingston cross the river to Hampton Wick (200m). At the road junction near the **White Hart** bear L past the drive from Home Park and cross to the side road R (50m).

⑪ Go along Church Grove (100m) and, opposite the church, take the footpath L to Bushy Park (250m).

⑫ Skirt round three sides of the sports field (350m) and follow the boundary to the next gate (200m). (Outside is the Cobbler's Memorial.)

⑬ Go L along Cobbler's Walk, the tarmac path from the gate, to the first footbridge (200m). Just before the bridge turn L onto the grass and follow paths L of the channels and ponds to the car park (1000m).

Kingston Bridge was the first above London Bridge until 1729 with great commercial significance and strategic importance at times of conflict. William IV opened the present bridge in 1828, one carriageway wide. It was freed of tolls in 1870. A second carriageway was added in 1914 and a third in 2000. The medieval timber bridge was 32m downstream (N). An order of Richard I in 1193 to repair it exists but the date of the first bridge is unknown. It was endowed in 1219 and 1565 to free it of tolls. To be rowed to Kingston Bridge from London cost 6s in 1770.

37 Bushy Park, Kingston and Teddington Lock

Read the note on the Royal Parks at the back. The route is blocked during the Hampton Court Flower Show. About 8½ km/5½ miles through the Royal Parks and along the Thames with a mile through Teddington to make the route circular. OS maps 1:25000 161 London South, 1:50000 176 West London

Start from the Diana Fountain car park in Bushy Park, TQ 160 693, or from the Hawker Centre in Kingston, TQ 177 712. Two train stations are near the route.

The Boaters ☎ 020 8541 4672
The Anglers ☎ 020 8977 7475
The Adelaide ☎ 020 8977 3616

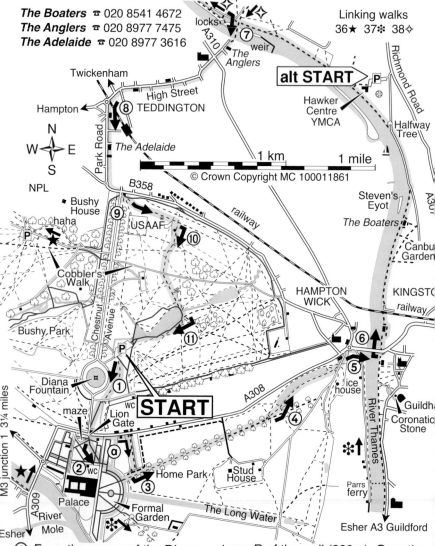

Linking walks
36★ 37✽ 38◇

① From the corner of the Diana Fountain car park near the car exit, take the hard path L & immediately diverge R over the grass to the trees R of the wall (300m). Over the tarmac drive, diverge R of the water channel to the gates of Bushy Park (250m). Cross the road. ✽

During BST, to avoid payment at the Formal Gardens ➔ⓐ. *In winter* ➔②

ⓐ Go L outside the wall to the Paddock Gate R after Ivy Cottage (300m) and take the path along the narrow field to Home Park (250m). Walk out from the wall into the avenue (30m). Turn L. ➔③

② Pass through the garden on the L diagonal path and enter the Formal Garden (200m). Cross to the water channel (50m). Follow it R (150m) and cross the first foot bridge. Go through the gateway into Home Park and ahead.

③ Keep to the avenue over the track from Stud House (700m) and on until two paths diverge L (300m).

④ Follow either diverging path to the pond (100m) and continue R of it to the end (400m) then up to the drive and the road exit L (200m).

⑤ Turn R along the main road and cross Kingston Bridge (250m). Drop R to the river bank.

⑥ Go under the bridge and carry on beside the Thames beneath the railway (250m), past the **Boaters** (600m), along the narrow road to the Half-mile Tree (650m) then on the footpath to Teddington Weir (900m) and footbridge (300m). Stay ahead to Teddington Lock (100m).✧ Cross the first lock gate to see the other locks then return to the footbridge (100m).

⑦ Cross the river to Teddington (150m). Stay ahead on the roads to the railway bridge at the top end of the High Street (1000m).

⑧ Go L along Park Road past the **Adelaide** (550m), round the bend (100m) and into Bushy Park R. ★

⑨ Turn L (20m). After the lodge (20m) diverge slightly R on the path which becomes parallel with the L wall 100m from it. Pass the white stone (USAAF memorial) (200m) and go on parallel with the wall, watching out for the gate L (100m).

⑩ Turn R on the cross path from the gate. Go past (L of) the SHAEF flagpole and plaque (50m) and on to the tarmac path, Cobbler's Walk (300m). Cross and continue ½L to the pond (300m).

⑪ Cross the water and go R along the bank to the car park (400m).

Ham, ton and wick are very common elements in place-names. They derive from Anglo-Saxon and mean more or less the same in translation whereas their combination in Hampton Wick suggests differences. *Tun* meant a homestead so became a part of the name of many farms or villages which grew into towns. *Wick*, cognate with Latin *vicus*, meant a hamlet or village sometimes best translated as *place* eg Norwich - north place; Gatwick - goat place. In Hampton, *wick* may have been appended to distinguish the early village from the manor. *Ham* is also best translated as homestead or farm and like *ton*, is common in farm and town names. However *hamm* was a wet place and is common near rivers. Hampton is more likely to mean *damp farm* than *farm farm*.

Norton, Sutton, Eaton and Weston are N,S,E & W place. Surbiton & Norbiton were S & N berewicks of Kingston. **~ing** as in Teddington is also very common (Woking, Padding, Sunning, Basing, Godalming) and derives from *~ingas* denoting the family group or band of the people who held the land early on during the Saxon settlement.

Ait and Eyot are alternative spellings for islet, of obscure origin. Saxon place-names associated with islands usually have the *y* sound, eg Eton, Chertsey, Molesey, Dorney.

38 Ham, Richmond Park and Teddington Lock

About 7½ km/4¾ miles with an extension of 2½ km/1½ miles to the Isabella Plantation (best for the Rhododendrons in May). Thames Path and park land. One stiff climb. OS maps 1:25000 161 London South, 1:50000 176 W London.

Start from the car park at Ham House, TQ 169 729, or Pembroke Lodge car park TQ 187 728. There is abundant kerbside parking in Riverside Drive, Ham. From Teddington the Thames footbridge gives access to the route.

The Dysart Arms ☎ 020 8940-8005
The Tap ☎ 020 8288 8699
Fox & Duck ☎ 020 8940 4944
New Inn ☎ 020 8940 9444

Linking walks 37✧ 39☆

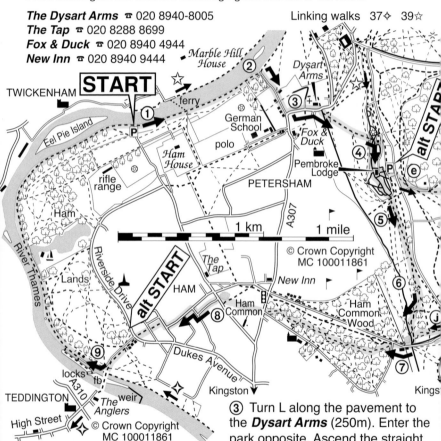

© Crown Copyright
MC 100011861

© Crown Copyright
MC 100011861

① At Ham House car park join the Thames towpath. Go R past Ham House R (150m), the Hammerton ferry landing (200m) ☆ and Marble Hill House L (80m). Keep on to the lane (500m). Up R is Richmond Hill and the Star & Garter Home.

② Turn R along the lane passing the Navigator's House R before the village street in Petersham (350m).

③ Turn L along the pavement to the **Dysart Arms** (250m). Enter the park opposite. Ascend the straight and steepest path (400m).

④ Enter the gardens. Ascend to the path on brow of the hill and go R to Pembroke Lodge (200m).

ⓔ *Extension of 2½ km/1½ miles: From the bottom end of Pembroke Lodge car park cross the road and the grass to the R corner of the wood (200m). Follow the tarmac drive L to the end (100m) then take the main path diverging from the wood, down through a belt of trees (200m) and on past the corner of a wood (250m) to Pen Ponds (500m) with White Lodge beyond.*

(f) Cross the isthmus dam between the ponds (300m).

(g) Turn R along the path beside the pond and carry on up round the wood to the road (650m).

(h) Go on beside the road to the oblique cross path ½L (250m). Follow it to the parking area of

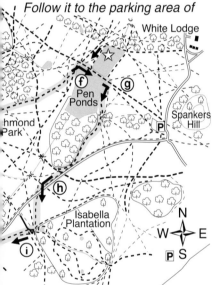

White Lodge

Pen Ponds

Spankers Hill

hmond Park

Isabella Plantation

N
W—E
S

P

the Isabella Plantation (300m).
(To see a bit of the plantation go round the pond and up the path beside the stream. If lost in the labyrinth, all downhill paths lead to the brooks and all brooks flow to the pond near the gate of entry.)

(i) Make for the car park exit drive, then bear L on the path converging on the road (300m). At the cross-roads, cross both roads R,L (50m).

(j) Walk along the track R of the steep road (50m) then fork R on the path to the brow of the hill (150m) and drop to the pond (100m). ➔(7)

(5) Carry on to the end gate of the garden (200m). Stay ahead on the brow of the hill to a mound (650m).

(6) At the next side path R (100m) diverge down to the pond (300m).

(7) Follow the road out of Ham Gate (50m). In wet seasons stay on the path beside the road. In summer, follow the winding path in the middle of the wood (not the horse track) L of the road. At the end of the wood (1000m) **New Inn** is R. Cross the main road and Ham Common (the village green) to the pond at the far L corner (350m). (The **Tap** is 150m beyond the pond.)

(8) Opposite the pond turn L along New Road to the end (200m) then R (50m) & L on Lock Road (200m). Turn R at the T-junction (40m) then L between the houses. Keep on in the same direction in passageways to Riverside Drive and open ground (Ham Lands) (200m). Go down the footpath to the River Thames at the Teddington footbridge (300m).◈

(9) Turn R to Teddington Lock (100m). Cross the first lock gate to see the lesser locks then continue on the river past the third lock gate (200m), Port of London obelisk L (250m), water sports lake R (400m) then opposite Twickenham and Eel Pie Island to the car park (1300m).

George **Vancouver**, 1758-1798, died while preparing reports at Navigator's House and is buried in Petersham churchyard. At 13 he was an able seaman on *Resolution* during Captain Cook's second voyage but rose to the rank of captain. On the way to accept Nootka Sound from Spain (by treaty) in 1791, he charted the Somebody-Knows-What coastline of Australia, the American coast northwards from San Francisco and Vancouver Island.

39 The Thames, Richmond Hill and Petersham

About 8 km/5 miles past Ham and Marble Hill Houses; a flat walk beside the river with one climb to Richmond Hill; across Hammerton Ferry (see note at back); a cultural detour in Twickenham and an extension of 4 km/2½ miles in Richmond Park. OS maps 1:25000 161 London South, 1:50000 176 W London.

Park below Twickenham Bridge in Ranelagh Drive, TQ 169 750, near the weir or at Pembroke Lodge car park in Richmond Park, TQ 187 728.

Linking walks 38☆ 40✳

Hammerton Ferry ☎ 020 8892 9620
The White Cross ☎ 020 8940 6844
The Roebuck ☎ 020 8948 2329
The Dysart Arms ☎ 020 8940 8005
The Fox & Duck ☎ 020 8940 4944
The White Swan ☎ 020 8892 2166

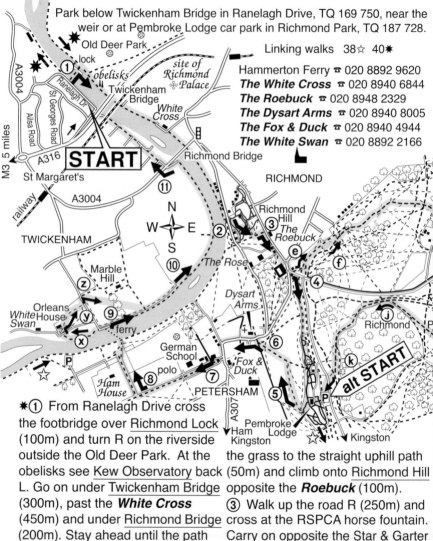

✳① From Ranelagh Drive cross the footbridge over Richmond Lock (100m) and turn R on the riverside outside the Old Deer Park. At the obelisks see Kew Observatory back L. Go on under Twickenham Bridge (300m), past the **White Cross** (450m) and under Richmond Bridge (200m). Stay ahead until the path bends L to the main road (550m).

② Cross into Terrace Garden opposite. Turn R up the side path above the road (100m), L up the edge of the garden (100m), R up the steps and exit R & up L. Cross the grass to the straight uphill path (50m) and climb onto Richmond Hill opposite the **Roebuck** (100m).

③ Walk up the road R (250m) and cross at the RSPCA horse fountain. Carry on opposite the Star & Garter Home and turn L into the gateway of Richmond Park (100m).

ⓔ *Extension of 4 km/2½ miles across Richmond Park: Go down the first side path L near the wall to the pond R (250m).*

(f) *Cross to the wide path on the opposite side of the pond (50m). Continue in the same direction winding down and up round to the fence above houses of Holly Lodge (800m). Stay ahead beside this and the iron fence of Two Storm Wood (700m). (The road ahead leads L to the Sheen Gate.)*

(g) *Turn R down the end fence and drop to the road (250m). Cross and carry on into the low grassy area between wooded slopes (350m).*

EAST SHEEN
P
(g)
Two Storms Wood
(h)
(i)
Pen Ponds
White Lodge

(h) *When level with the wood up R, bear R on the oblique path skirting the lower trees (350m). Cross the track from White Lodge L and go on above the Pen Pond (400m).* ☆

(i) *Turn R up the track from between the ponds, rising straight to the top of the ridge at the R edge of the fenced wood near the road (900m).*

(j) *Carry on round the wood until level with the mound in the wood L and the thatched cottage R (600m).*

(k) *Bear R aross the grass to the Pembroke Lodge car park. Go into the garden and round the house to the terrace (300m).* ➡(5)

(4) Turn R along the fence (450m). Stay on the brow of the hill through the garden to Pembroke Lodge (with restaurant) (450m). ☆

(5) From the terrace drop to the fence and gate (50m) then descend ½R through the park to the gate opposite the **Dysart Arms** in Petersham (500m).

(6) Cross to the pavement and go L through the village (100m). (The church R has interesting graves. Vancouver's grave is at the S wall of the graveyard.) Carry on along the village street round the L bend to the **Fox & Duck** (250m).

(7) Opposite the pub enter the German School drive and join the path between the two drives behind the lodge. Follow the path between the drives (300m) and carry on beside the polo field to the garden wall of Ham House (350m).

(8) Turn R on the path along the wall (300m). At the end bear slightly R to the river (100m). Cross by the Hammerton Ferry.

(x) *Detour of 700m/½ mile: Go L along the river bank and round the L edge of the little park (300m).*

(y) *At the lane cross into the small gate of Orleans House. Walk past the door then follow paths towards the far R corner of the grounds and the exit gate in the wall (250m).*

(z) *Go L along the lane and R into the park (60m). Cut diagonally over the grass to the main gate at the river (450m). Turn L.* ➡(10)

(9) Follow the riverbank R past Marble Hill House far L (350m).

(10) Stay on the river bank to Richmond Bridge (1200m).

(11) Turn L up to the main road and cross to the 1st side road R (100m). Follow Willoughby Road then stay ahead on paths and roads under Twickenham Bridge to Ranelagh Drive and Richmond Weir (900m).

40 Richmond Lock, Syon Park and Kew Bridge

About 10 km/6¼ miles; a flat walk beside the Thames but numerous flights of steps. OS maps 1:25000 161 London South, 1:50000 176 West London

Park at the weir in Ranelagh Drive, TQ 169 750, near Twickenham Bridge or at Isleworth Church. Kew Bridge Station is closest to the route.

Town Wharf ☎ 020 8847 2287   Linking walk 71✱
London Apprentice ☎ 020 8560 1915
Rose & Crown ☎ 020 8334 1030
Butterfly House
     ☎ 020 8560 7272

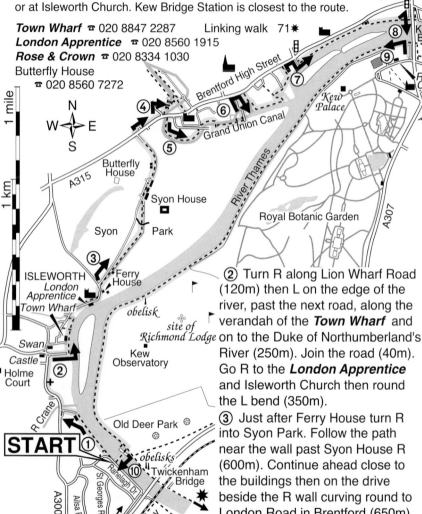

② Turn R along Lion Wharf Road (120m) then L on the edge of the river, past the next road, along the verandah of the **Town Wharf** and on to the Duke of Northumberland's River (250m). Join the road (40m). Go R to the **London Apprentice** and Isleworth Church then round the L bend (350m).

③ Just after Ferry House turn R into Syon Park. Follow the path near the wall past Syon House R (600m). Continue ahead close to the buildings then on the drive beside the R wall curving round to London Road in Brentford (650m).

④ Cross and go R beside the road to the Grand Union Canal (200m). Descend L of the bridge to the canal (50m). Cross the footbridge over both locks and the next footbridge R (50m). Stay ahead to High Street and cross to the church (100m). Turn R to the canal (50m).

① From Richmond Lock follow the riverside away from Twickenham Bridge (50m) and continue on the footpath (350m). Keep on to the road (100m) then R, over the River Crane, to the T-junction (400m).

⑤ At the bridge, drop to the canal L and follow it, curving L (400m). Turn L under the bridge to the road then rejoin the canal R and carry on to the footbridge (100m). Cross then drop to the canal. Keep on to Thames Lock (250m).

⑥ Climb the steps to the bridge. Cross the canal L and continue to Brentford High Street (150m). Turn R (60m) and R again back to the canal (100m). Follow the bank L (250m). Zigzag LR round the inlet and continue down-river until forced back to the road (350m).

⑦ Go R to the main road junction (100m) then R between the buildings (20m). Pass through the wall L and re-join the river bank (30m). Carry on, over a building, and all the way to Kew Bridge (with a brief return to the road) (900m).

⑧ Cross the river. Continue to the crossroads and Kew Green (300m).

⑨ Double back beside the bridge to the river bank (100m). Turn L. Stay on the riverside path all the way back, past Kew Palace L (600m), Brentford Gate of Kew Gardens L opposite the canal R (300m), Syon House R (800m), an obelisk for Kew Observatory L (900m), Isleworth Church (250m) to Richmond Lock (1000m).

⑩ Cross the footbridge over the lock to Ranelagh Drive (100m).

The **Grand Union Canal** had immense importance linking the industrial heart of the Empire in the Midlands with London, the largest port. When built it was the Grand Junction Canal to Braunston, 90 miles long with 100 locks. Digging started at both ends in 1793. The first section, Brentford to Uxbridge, opened in 1794. Combining with other canals it became the Grand Union in 1928.

Isleworth is GILSTELESWORDE in the Domesday Book, a manor of 70 hides but there was a Gisleresuuyrth in a forged charter for a grant of land in 677 by Bishop Eorcenwold to Barking Abbey from king Ethelred of Mercia (674-704). Henry V gave the manor to the community of St Bridget (English Bridgettines) to expiate his father's role in Richard II's death. J M W Turner lived at Ferry House 1804-06. Before taking up painting, Vincent van Goch taught at Holme Court when it was a school. The church, All Saints, was burnt down during WWII by schoolboys; only the tower is ancient. The Duke of Northumberland's River was originally the Bourne but was augmented by a cut from the River Crane to power new mills which became an industrial centre for brass, calico and dyes. The dock shipped the product of the Hounslow Heath gunpowder works and was always important for boat building.

Syon Park (☎ 020 8560 0882) home of the Dukes of Northumberland, is the only ancient noble seat still in London. It was the site of Syon Abbey of the English Brigettines who moved to Isleworth in 1431 and were suppressed in 1539. In the confiscated abbey Catherine Howard was kept for execution, dogs licked the blood from Henry VIII's coffin and Lady Jane Grey agreed to become queen. Protector Somerset acquired the estate in 1547 and built the Tudor house before losing his head. Henry Percy, the 9th Earl of Northumberland married into it in 1594. Canaletto painted the house in 1752.

Kew Bridge was opened in 1903 by Edward VII. The first bridge was built of timber a little downriver as a private enterprise by Robert Tunstall in 1759. He replaced this with a stone bridge in 1789. It cost £57,000 to extinguish the tolls in 1876. A sheep was roasted on the river here when it froze in 1788. The thaw was so abrupt, pieces of ice of a ton were thrown up to 100 feet from the river.

Anthony's is the cluster of houses at the NE corner of Horsell Common. There used to be five Chertsey almshouses there and, around 1850 an Anthony Ives lived in one of them. Perhaps people went to Anthony's.

The Round **Barrows** of Surrey are Bronze Age burial mounds. They appeared all over Europe around 2600 BC and had a dagger and beaker buried with the body. Later in the Bronze Age cremation became the norm and urns with ashes are found under the mounds. About 100 are known in Surrey but many will have disappeared through gravel extraction, ploughing etc. The Horsell Common bell barrow, dated 1400-1200 BC, late Bronze Age, still has its ditch.

The **Basingstoke Canal** is 37 miles long. It started from the Wey Navigation at Byfleet in 1796 at the apogee of the canal building period. Not linking areas of industry and dense population it was perceived as the first agricultural canal - food to London; coal and horse dung to the country - but it did not pay for itself. The peak year for traffic was 1838 when the railway was built. The last barge tied up at Basingstoke in 1910. The canal is now owned by Surrey and Hants County Councils. Cut by the M3, it is navigable only as far as Odiham Castle.

London's lost route to Basingstoke P A L Vine 1968   David & Charles 212pp

The **Beacon** on Wisley Airfield is a VHF Omnidirectional Rangefinder, VOR. An aircraft detects its exact position from it without reference to any other beacon. There are about 50 such beacons in Britain and the chief aircraft lanes cross them. This VOR is also the centre for one of Heathrow's four stacking circuits.

The **Bee Gardens** on Chobham Common are ancient earthworks of unknown age and use. They may have been convenient markers for positioning hives in summer, but it is unlikely they were constructed for this. The smaller, near the east boundary, appears to be a moated enclosure and probably held a house. The larger encloses about 2 acres and might have been a corral for livestock.

Bisley was listed as part of Chobham in a Chertsey Abbey charter of 933. The name was spelt *Busselegh* which may derive from 'bushy clearing'. The tenant of 1284 held the estate as a parcel of Byfleet and was patron of its church. The little church, St John the Baptist, has nave walls of puddingstone and heath stone which probably date from about that time. Bisley is known throughout the world for shooting. Besides hosting national and international competitions it is home to about 30 shooting clubs for a wide range of small arms. The NFA National Rifle Association was formed in 1860 having roots in the Volunteers. It was pushed out of Wimbledon Common by the growth of London and acquired Bisley Common in 1890. The army paid and have retained the ranges ever since but the clubs have their own buildings . The NRA has a museum open two days a week (☎ 01483-797777 ext 125). In the early days the NRA had its own railway - the bridge pillars still stand near Lock 15.

The **Bourne** starts as trickles on Bagshot Heath and Chobham Ridges which become the Windle Brook then the Millbourne of Chobham. It collects the outflow from Virginia Water and flows beside Chertsey Meads to the Thames.

Brentford is at the lowest fordable point on the Thames. Julius Cæsar is said to have crossed here with his legions but other places make the same claim. It was one of the earliest suburbs to reach out from the City. Brentford's greatest gift to the nation was probably John Wilkes, the great reforming influence who was returned to Parliament for Middlesex in 1765 mainly by Brentford voters.

Broadmead was the medieval common pasture of 365 acres with about 50 owners in the 19th century. It was open for grazing by the commoners of Send and Woking from September 18th to March, the rest of the year being for hay.

Brook Place, a fine Dutch-style house, is an ecumenical conference centre and retreat. The house was built in 1656 by William Beauchamp. The previous house belonged to Edward Bray who was awarded the property by Charles I for raising a troup of horse. Chertsey Abbey's manorial records for Chobham show a William de Broke deprived of his tenancy for poor farming in 1302.

Brookwood is a narrow strip between the Basingstoke Canal and the railway which grew at the extremity of Woking parish because of the cemetery. The station was interpolated in 1864 at the junction of the cemetery's private line.

Bushy House was built for Charles II's keeper of the Middle Park and was the home of the Earls of Halifax when they were Rangers. William IV (third son of George III) lived there. The Greek temple in the garden is the sailor king's monument to Nelson - a close friend. In 1900 Bushy House became the HQ and Director's House for NPL, the National Physical Laboratory.

Bushy Park has free car parks. Chestnut Avenue is used as a public road. The Sunday closest to May 11th every year is Chestnut Sunday when the trees are in flower and a fête is held. The park was put together for Cardinal Wolsey when he built Hampton Court Palace. It still has deer, the numbers being kept at about 125 red and 200 fallow. The water channels are the artificial Longford River dug from the Colne River for Charles I to bring clean water to Hampton Court Palace. The Diana Fountain was probably commissioned by Charles I for Somerset House but may be Arethusa. Cobbler's Walk commemorates Timothy Bennett, a shoe-maker of Hampton Wick, who threatened the Earl of Halifax, Ranger, with litigation for closing the path in 1752, since when it has been a public right of way. There is a memorial to him outside Hampton Wick Gate. During World War II the US Army & Airforce had its HQ in Bushy Park (Camp Griffiss), 1942-44 and for three months in 1944 General Eisenhower had SHAEF (Supreme HQ Allied Expeditionary Forces) there planning D-Day.

Byfleet village expanded towards Woking and became part of the borough in 1933 at the same time as Pyrford. In the Domesday Book it was BIFLET with a church, a mill and fishery taxed @ 325 eels. Edward II acquired it from the abbey and gave it to Piers Gaveston. Later it was owned by the Black Prince and documents signed here show he visited, probably to hunt in the forest. The church, St Mary's, is the medieval church with a Victorian church tacked on. The old part may be on the site of the Domesday Book church but was built around 1300. Points of interest: the roofs; brass of Thomas Teylar, Rector 1454-1489, stones in the old walls. West Byfleet took its name from the station.

Byfleet Manor House was built in the 1620s for Anne of Denmark, Queen to James I, and the gate pillars date from that time. It has been rebuilt several times but is still a Jacobean mansion.

Chertsey is in Runnymede Borough with Virginia Water, Englefield Green, Egham, Thorpe, Addlestone and Ottershaw. It had an abbey founded in 666, destroyed by the Vikings and restarted, ending only with the Dissolution in 1537 (see box p 3). In 731 Bede wrote of the founding and explained CERATÆSEI meant Cerot's Island. It was CERTSEY in the Domesday Book.

Chertsey Bridge is an elegant Georgian link between the town and Middlesex though Pevsner thinks the arches do not fit well with the triangular profile. It was built a few yards upsteam of the old timber bridge in 1785. The earliest known bridge was licensed in 1410 by Henry IV. Sibille the ferrywomen was paid 3 shillings for transporting the king and family in 1299. Dickens has Oliver Twist crossing it with Sykes on his way to be initiated as a burglar.

Chobham was Chebeham, one of the earliest places known from the charter of 673 (see box p3). It was probably the home of a Saxon called Ceabba which is the diminutive of Cædbæd. In the Domesday book it is CEBEHÁ, listed as having a church. Henry VIII took the manor for himself at the dissolution of the abbey in 1537. The demesne was imparked around 1558 becoming Chobham Park. Queen Mary sold that to Nicholas Heath, Archbishop of York. Although he proclaimed Queen Elizabeth (1558) he refused to crown her and spent the next decade in the Tower for denying church decrees. Later lords of the manor have been the Mores of Loseley, the Zouches of Bramshill and the Onslows of Clandon. The church, St Lawrence, stands on a Saxon site. The Papal licence to bury the dead was granted in 1215; Chertsey Abbey's compensation for loss of trade was 20s and 6 lbs of beeswax p.a. Features of interest: the Norman chalk pillars of the south aisle with fluted capitals of around 1150, the tops of the earlier windows of about 1080 above them and the elbow beams; the chest of around 1250; 16th century wooden font; tower of around 1400; north aisle pillars of 1886; the memorial screen for two World Wars at the door; the plaque about Archbishop Heath near the chancel arch and his burial place (blue marble stone before the altar), the puddingstone and heathstone external walls.

The History of Chobham R Schueller 1989 Phillimore 203pp

Chobham Common, presently 1445 acres, was bought by Surrey CC in 1986 @ £1 per acre and is now maintained by Surrey Wildlife Trust. Most is heath. Marsh gentian and sundew grow in some of the marshy places and Deptford pinks on high parts. *Sphagnum* moss was harvested in WWI for wound dressing like cottonwool. The Battle of Wibandun in 586 may have been fought here. Wimbledon claims the battle but there was a place called Wipsedone in the Chertsey Abbey boundary list attached to the Charter of 673. This is the first battle recorded between Saxons in the Anglo-Saxon Chronicle. Apparently King Ethelbert of Kent was trying to expand which brought him into conflict with Cealwin of the West Saxons and he was driven back "even as far as Kent". The princes Oslaf and Chebba were killed. Chobham Common, like other SE heaths, has been used for army training camps. The 1853 camp was the last before the army went into permanent camp on the heath at Aldershot. The *London Illustrated News* reported 8129 men, 1508 horses and 24 guns took part. *Punch* poked fun. Queen Victoria reviewed the troops as written on the stone near Monument car park. The allotment movement appears to have started on the Common for Lord Onslow leased small plots to soldiers returning from the Napoleonic Wars @ 2 shillings per acre p.a. and moved the Allotment Act of 1831. The leases for brick clay pits given by Lord Onslow brought him into conflict with the commoners in one of only two cases of litigation against a Lord of the Manor (1870). The outcome was a compromise in which Lord Onslow received 200 acres of the Common and agreed not to issue leases for clay digging. The 200 acres became building land for Sunningdale.

A History of Chobham Common Joy Mason 1994 31p

Coal Tax Posts marked the tax boundary at roads, canals and rivers. 219 are known. After the Fire of London a tax was imposed on coal brought into London to pay for the rebuilding. Like other taxes it remained in force beyond the original remit. The Coal and Wine Tax Act of 1862 equated the tax zone with the Metropolitan Police District - the Middlesex border in the west. The post at the retail car park in Staines is beside the towpath where the river crosses from Berkshire (Buckinghamshire until 1974) into Middlesex on the opposite bank.

Cobham appears as Getinges in the early charter of 673 when it was given to Chertsey Abbey as an estate of 10 mansae of land. An early form of the present name was COVEHAM, probably deriving from *Cofa*, a person's name + ham or Cove a bend in the river + hamm. Edward the Confessor added to the estate; the Domesday Book manor of COVENHAM was taxed for 30 hides before the Conquest. Cobham Court was the later manor house. Cobham Park was earlier called Downe Place after its owner. The town owes much to its position on the River Mole and the London-Portsmouth road. In 1793 it had its own London coach, out at 7am, back at 6 pm; 4 shillings inside. 2 shillings outside. Its part in retail history is that it had the first self-service Woolworth. The church, St Andrew is the product of much rebuilding but the base of the tower and (re-positioned) main door are 12th century. The first recorded rector was Aymer around 1166.   *Cobham - a history* David Taylor 2003 Phillimore 150p

Cowey Stakes is the side of the Thames between Walton Bridge and the Desborough Cut. Stakes are found in the river bed. Here, some claim, Julius Caesar's army crossed the Thames during his second expedition to Britain. The name is said to derive from a ford marked by stakes for drovers.

A **Curfew Bell** rings at Chertsey church at 8pm. Neville Audley took sanctuary in the abbey to avoid execution after the Lancastrian defeat in the Battle of Barnet. Yorkists threatened the abbey so, expecting a reprieve, he promised to emerge at curfew. The king's messenger was delayed at the ferry and Neville's lover Blanche Heriot clung to the clapper to stop the curfew bell ringing. This is a myth deriving from a play of 1842 by Albert Smith and popularised 10 years later by Rose Harwick's poem, *Curfew must not ring tonight*, re-set in the Civil War, with reprieve from Cromwell.   *Tales of Old Surrey* Matthew Alexander 1985

The **Desborough Cut** was made in 1935 and the land enclosed within the meanders of the river became Desborough Island. Lord Desborough was the president of the Thames Conservancy at the time.

Emmetts Mill on the Mill Bourne is a residence made from the 18th century millhouse where stood a 14th century abbey mill. Emmett was miller in 1577.

Fairoaks Aerodrome was a farmer's private airstrip in the 1930s and became Dolley's Farm flying station in World War II for initial pilot training in Tiger Moths. The RAF retained it until 1966 and the runway was grass until 1978. It is now an aviation business complex with commercial airport for light aircraft.
     Surrey Airfields in the Second World War Len Pilkington Countryside Books 1997

The **fishponds** were probably part of the fish farm dug by Chertsey Abbey when Rutherwyke was Abbott 1307-40. Gracious Pond near the bend in the lane was filled in around 1870. Gracious Pond Farmhouse may be on the site of the piscatorial brothers' house. *Gracious* may be derived from a person's name for it was Cratchette's pond in 1461.

The **German School** in Petersham occupies the grounds of Douglas House. The original house is the admin section and takes its name from Kitty Douglas, Countess of Queensbury, the great patron of artists. She built a summer house for John Gay on the river bank and *The Beggars Opera* was rehearsed here. The school is now independent but was started by the German Government for Germans working in London. It has about 600 children, ages 5-19.

Goldsworth was a hamlet which gave its name to the most outlying tithing of Woking Parish which also included the hamlets of Brookwood and Knaphill. It was *Goldhord* in a deed of 1229 which suggests the origin of the name.

Gordon's School was founded in 1885 as a memorial to the general killed the same year in Khartoum. Initially it provided artisan training for boys who had left school at 14, to fit them for civilian or military life. Now it is a minor public school with 650 boys and girls. A statue of Gordon on a camel is visible from the Chobham road - repatriated by the Sudanese at Independence.

Gordon and the Gordon Boys School Lt Col G S Hutchinson 1944 GBS 56pp

Ham is ESTRAHÃ in the Domesday Book, a small estate held from Chertsey Abbey by sheriff Hamo. It was part of the crown lands of Saxon Kingston.

Ham House (☎ 020 8940 1950) has been owned by the National Trust since 1948. The present form and furnishing is largely due to Elizabeth Murray, a formidable dame, who provided intelligence for Charles II in exile and became Countess Dysart in her own right. She received the Ham and Petersham estate as her marriage portion from her father who had been a childhood companion of Charles I. From her first marriage to Sir Lionel Tollmarche derive the family who owned the house until 1948. Her second husband was the Duke of Lauderdale - the L in Charles II's CABAL.

The **Hammerton Ferry** between Ham and Marble Hill is the only small ferry on the tidal part of the Thames. It operates weekends throughout the year 10-6.30 but weekdays only Feb-Oct 10-6. It was started by Walter Hammerton in 1908. Lord Dysart claimed a monopoly but was defeated in the House of Lords.

Hampton was a great royal manor of 35 hides listed in the Middlesex folios of the Domesday Book which included the land now under Twickenham. The first church was put up in 1342 by Takeley Priory. The present building is too plain for a Victorian church and indeed was built in 1831. The crown on the flagstaff denotes the royal connection; the monarch has presented the vicars since the dissolution. Pevsner says of it: "nothing mysterious, nothing enthusiastic".

Hampton Court Palace is open to the public; the ticket office is on the west side. The Formal Garden is free in winter but has an entry charge during BST. The palace was built around the manor house of the Knights Hospitallers of St John who held the manor from 1236. Cardinal Wolsey leased the estate and built himself a great palace starting in 1515 when he became Lord Chancellor and Papal legate. It had a staff of 500 and 280 rooms reserved for visitors. Falling foul of the king, he made a placatory gift of the palace to Henry VIII in 1527 who used it as one of his principal family homes and made substantial alterations. Edward VI was born here. Queens Mary and Elizabeth held court here. The authorised version of the Bible was the outcome of a conference held by James I here. After the Civil War, a valuation was made for demolishing the palace and selling the scrap but, when made Lord Protector, Cromwell decided to live there. It was the main home of William and Mary; William was asthmatic and refused to stay at Whitehall Palace. Queen Victoria opened it to the public. The Great Gate House (west side), originally two storeys taller, and the buildings around Base Court, behind it, were Wolsey's but most of his palace has been superseded. The wings were added for Henry VIII about 1536. The King's Beasts on the bridge and the brick chimneys are modern copies. Anne Boleyn's Gateway into Clock Court can be seen through the main gateway. The main block facing the Formal Garden is the brick and Portland Stone palace built for William & Mary by Sir Christopher Wren who worked on it into his 80s. Parts of the palace and houses on the estate are grace & favour residences in the gift of the crown. The 2nd and 4th house along Hampton Road opposite Trophy Gate were the final homes of Wren and Faraday.

Hampton Court Palace June Osborne HMSO 1984 224pp

Heath occurs in low rainfall areas on sandy soils deficient in calcium - badland caused through oak deforestation by farmers as early as the Neolithic. Humus does not gel on the sand particles in the absence of calcium so the soil does not hold enough water, nutrients and microbes to sustain many species. Only a specialized flora can survive: heathers, bracken, gorse. In this area the Tertiary (Bagshot) Sands and Ice Age river gravels underlie the dry soils.

Heathstone is the grey stone with glinting quartz grains seen in old churches in the Woking area, the large blocks of the Virginia Water cascade and coping stones of the Basingstoke Canal locks. It formed beds in the upper Tertiary Sands of the Chobham and Bagshot heaths which have been stripped. The rounded blocks left exposed on the surface by erosion are sarsens. In this rock deficient area sarsens were used for church foundations and boundary marks.

Horsell Common is open to the public for recreational use but is private land owned by its Preservation Society. Until the start of the 20th century it was regulated and used like other commons but in 1910 the lord of the manor, Lord Onslow, put its management in the hands of a group of residents who became trustees. They bought the freehold in 1960 and registered the society in 1961. About half the 810 acres are an SSSI. Horsell was part of the Pyrford manor from Domesday Book times until 1815. It has an ancient parish church but no "big house". The church has features dated to 1320 but may be older for Newark Abbey was granted the advowson in 1258. The village expanded at the same time as Woking and merged with Woking UDC in 1907.

Kew Royal Botanic **Gardens** (020 8332 5655) started as a strip of ornamental gardens along the Thames from Richmond Lodge in which George, Prince of Wales, escaped the court of George I. The next Prince of Wales, Frederick, leased an estate beside it and had a house (White Palace, demolished) near Dutch House. His wife and widow Princess Augusta and her mentor, Lord Bute (3rd Earl) collected novel plants and had the Pagoda built by William Chambers in 1761 at the height of the interest in Chinese art. George III bought the estate and united it with the Richmond gardens. Other houses and gardens, eg Dutch House of 1631 (now called Kew Palace), were incorporated. Sir Joseph Banks was *de facto* director. Later on Kew pioneered the transfer of crops throughout the Empire and became a repository for botanical knowledge with a herbarium and laboratories. George III was incarcerated at "Kew Palace" during his periods of madness. Kew - History of the Royal Botanic Gardens R Desmond 1995

Kew Observatory was built for George III near his house Richmond Lodge for the transit of Venus across the Sun in 1780. He took great interest in time measurement and used the observatory as the hub of British time. Clocks were tested against one another and against astronomic observations. It was here that John Harrison brought his longitude-measuring Chronometer V for trials by George III. The obelisks near the Thames N & S of the observatory were for aligning instruments. Thermometers and barometers were calibrated and the first British seismometer installed (1898). The British Association for Advancement of Science acquired the observatory in 1840 from which it passed to the Royal Society. It became the National Physical Laboratory in 1900. That moved to Bushy House after a few months but kept the observatory as a department until 1980. Most Government science establishments were spawned from NPL so Kew Observatory was their progenitor.   *Longitude*   Dava Sobel 1998 Fourth Estate

Kingston is the county capital but as a London borough is not administratively part of Surrey. Its early significance was as the meeting place between the Kingdom of Wessex and the London area. At the Council of Kingston in 838 the Wessex king, Egbert, gave back land to the Archbishop of Canterbury in exchange for support of his heirs. This established the first stable Saxon dynasty; Alfred the Great was Egbert's grandson. Alfred's son, Edward the Elder was crowned (901) at the Coronation Stone, now near the Guild Hall, and so were the next six kings. Between them they resisted then absorbed the Danes and united the whole of England for the first time. Kingston received its Borough charter from King John in 1200 but already had town officers when CHINGESTVN was listed in the Domesday Book - a large manor in the King's demesne. The church, All Saints, largely rebuilt in the mid-19th century, has fabric dating back to the 13th century and may be on the site of the Saxon church listed in the Domesday Book. The Italianate Market Hall was the Townhall 1840 -1935. The medieval Bishops of Winchester had a large house between the market place and the river.

Lock 15 on the Basingstoke Canal is the first of the steep Deepcut series, climbing 29m/95 feet to Lock 28. The nearby pillars were for the Bisley Railway.

The **London - Southampton** railway line: see box on page 39.

Longcross may get its name from a cross marking the boundary for Chertsey, Egham and Chobham. A hamlet of Chertsey, it became a parish in 1847 when the landowner William Tringham built the church to save his neighbours and workers the journey to Chertsey. He was not all good for he also bought the two public houses and extinguished their licences. He built the first Longcross House; the present house dates from 1994. The church is unusual in lying on a north-south axis.   *The story of Longcross* H J F Tringham 1934 24pp

Marble Hill House (☎ 020 8892 5115) was completed in 1729 and is one of the most perfect Palladian houses in England; it also contains a fine collection of furniture of the period. It was built for Henrietta Howard, Duchess of Suffolk, mistress of George II. The initial design was by Colen Campbell who brought the Palladian style to England. The impoverished Duke of Suffolk anticipating the accession of George I moved to Hanover and became a Groom of the Bedchamber. His young Duchess caught the eye of the soon-to-be Prince of Wales. The prince paid £12000 towards the house; the duke received an annuity of £1200.   *Marble Hill* Julius Bryant 2002   40pp

The **McLaren** building opened in 2003, is the HQ of the TAG-McLaren Group housing all company activities, research, factory, training, admin and museum. It replaced 18 buildings mainly in the Woking area. McLarens only develop and build racing cars though sister companies develop and sell electronic equipment for vehicles and leisure.

Mimbridge appears as a boundary mark for Chobham with Chertsey Abbey's 13th century copy of the charter of about 673. The name may derive from *mint*.
The Place-Names of Surrey J E B Gover, A Mawer & F M Stenton 1934 CUP

The River **Mole** rises near Gatwick airport where it is culverted under the runway. It cuts through the North Downs at Dorking where part of its course is underground via several swallow holes in the chalk. It drains to the Thames opposite Hampton Court at Molesey, from which it derives its present-day name. The earlier name, *Emel*, survives in Elmbridge.

Molesey Lock opened 1815 (rebuilt 1906), the weir being to raise water over shoals upstream. The first keeper, John Nash, "citizen and butcher" was paid 35s weekly and was killed by a racehorse in Hurst Park. Molesey was part of the bequest to Chertsey Abbey in the charter of 673, Muleseie in 727.

The **Monastery** in Brookwood Cemetery of the Brotherhood of St Edward the Martyr occupies the original Anglican chapel of the cemetery and its church was the second Anglican chapel. The adjacent raised areas are the remains of the platform of the cemetery railway terminus. The monastery was created in 1984 as a shrine and chantry for St Edward and to service the church for the Orthodox community. Edward was the Saxon king of all England, 975-979, after the death of his father, Edgar, and was crowned at Kingston. His bones were found at Shaftesbury Abbey by archæologists in 1931 and after theft and legal wrangling were brought here. *The Criminologist* Vol 5, Nos 16/17 May/August 1970

The **Muslim Cemetery** was started in 1915 to counter German disinformation that sepoys were not receiving proper death rites. The 28 were re-interred in Brookwood cemetery in 1969. Hindu sepoys were cremated at Brighton.

NPL, the National Physical Laboratory, came about when the Royal Society expanded out of Kew Observatory to provide premises for devising accurate standard measurements. The first lab was in Bushy House but numerous government funded blocks were added (and demolished) over the years for aircraft, ships, electricity, optics, metallurgy, DNA, the Government Chemist, etc. This is where RADAR started (1938), the first atomic clock, the first stored memory computer (1949). The prototype Spitfire was tested in the wind tunnels; the bouncing bomb was tested in the ship tanks. Many Government research labs were spawned from NPL: National Engineering at East Kilbride, Hydraulics at Wallingford, Building at Watford, Road at Crowthorne, Paint at Teddington, Fire at Elstree, Radio at Slough, Radar at Worcester and various Commonwealth standards offices.

The **Nauticalia Ferry** between Shepperton and Weybridge crosses on the half hour but continuously when busy. Weekdays 8-6; weekends 9-5. It can cease to operate for several days when the Thames is in spate. This is where the towing path changed sides so the Nauticalia boatmen are of antique lineage.

Newark Mill was a timber building with three wheels but burned down in 1966. It was probably on the site of the Domesday Book Send mill taxed for 21s 6d.

Newark Priory was initiated by Ruald de Calric during the reign (1189-99) of Richard the Lionheart. It was a new place for the Augustinian canons. The building is 13th century but overlies an earlier church. It was endowed with gifts of land round about and in London, whose ownership is still remembered in place names with *priory,* eg at Hurtmore and Puttenham. It also held the advowsons of many local churches and provided their vicars eg Windlesham, Send, Horsell, Pyrford, Pirbright, Woking, West Clandon and St Martha's.

Occam's Razor is now a saw of science. William of Occam (1290?-1349) is thought to have originated from the village which attracts visitors from all over the world because of him. A friar, educated at the Franciscan house in Oxford, he taught at the University of Paris and figures in the development of logic, philosophy and political theory. As an ecclesiastical rebel he was a fore-runner of Martin Luther (1483-1546) leading a splinter group of Franciscans who demanded evangelical poverty. He accused Pope John XII of 70 errors and 7 heresies and was excommunicated in 1330. Aided and protected by the Holy Roman Emperor, the Bavarian, Louis IV, he escaped house arrest at Avignon and spent the rest of his life in Munich where he is commemorated by Occamstraße. The razor is: *Entia non sunt multiplicanda præter necessitatem* - entities are not to be multiplied without necessity. In science, if more than one explanations is possible, the simplest is best until evidence contradicts it.

Ockham was a traditional English estate until the demise of the Lovelace family after WWII. The land and all the houses belonged to the Lord of the Manor and it was self sufficient with a building and maintenance department, home farm, mill, church and manor house. The village is small - a few cottages along the roads. The Earls of Lovelace were lineal descendants of Peter King, Lord Chancellor (1725), who bought the estate in 1710. It was was BOCHEHÃ In the Domesday Book, with a clerical error, B. William the Conqueror gave it to his soldier, Richard FitzGilbert. The church, All Saints, may have some of the fabric of the Domesday Book church but the greater part of the nave and chancel walls date from around 1220. It is a typical village church with many alterations from later periods. Features of interest: the 7-lancet east window, of around 1250; the monument to Lord King in the King chapel; the ceilings with all the roof bosses different; the doorway of the rood loft high up beside the chancel arch; the 3-course tower c1500; the west window of the north aisle commemorating the 700th anniversary of the birth of William of Ockham.

Ockham Mill is now a residence with the splendid brickwork favoured by the Lovelaces of the Ockham estate. The building dates from 1862; milling ceased in 1927. The wheel is internal, 14' 6" diameter, 9' 10" wide. There has been a mill here since at least 1296. *Watermills of Surrey* Derek Stidder 1990 Barracuda Books

Ockham Park house was built in 1629 for Henry Weston. This Jacobean house was transformed under the direction of Nicholas Hawksmoor into an Italianate mansion in the 1830s. The main house has been rebuilt since the serious fire of 1948 but the stable and orangery are as before.

Orleans House Gallery Twickenham (☎ 020 8831 6000) has free admission. It is the most important fine art collection in London after the national collections - chiefly relating to local scenes or people. The house was built in 1710 for James Johnson, Secretary of State for Scotland under William III. The Duc d'Orleans of the exiled French royal family lived there 1815-17.

Ottershaw Park is now apartments but has been Ottershaw College and the Mobiloil HQ. It was built in 1908 on the site of an earlier house. Lord Brabazon, later 12th Earl of Meath leased the park in the 1880s when the Countess associated herself with the initiation of the Meath Home at Godalming.

Petersham, in the Borough of Richmond, has been a prestigious domicile from early times because of the Thames which provided rapid transport and later because of the proximity of various royal households and the beauty of the landscape. It has grand houses of numerous noble families and courtiers. Charles Dickens wrote Nicholas Nickleby at Elm Lodge. The first reference, in the dubious copy of a charter of 727 is Piterichesham, a bequest of 10 mansæ of land to Chertsey Abbey by sub-king Frithwold of Surrey. This was 10 hides of PATRICESHÄ in the Domesday Book when the rent included 1000 eels and 1000 lampreys. The manor was transferred to the Crown in 1415 and annexed to Sheen (Richmond). Henry VIII settled it on Anne of Cleves for life after the divorce, to be leased for income. It became part of the estate of James I's son Henry Prince of Wales (who died early) and was eventually given to the Earl of Dysart, William Murray (whipping boy of Charles I) for his daughter Elizabeth.

The **pillboxes** are World War II relics of the GHQ line which stretched from the Medway to near Gloucester to defend London and the Midlands. The line follows natural obstacles such as the Downs, canals and rivers.

Pillboxes - a study of UK defences 1940 Henry Wills 1985 Secker & Warburg 98pp

Pirbright was not a Domesday Book manor but was probably cut from Woking Manor by Henry I for his son Robert, Duke of Gloucester. The last notable Lord of the Manor, Lord Pirbright, lived at Henley Park. Many pre-WWI cottages, bear the estate logo. The village hall on the green was a gift of Lord Pirbright. The church, St Michael and All Angels, with heathstone tower is Georgian but there was a church by 1200, deduced from a charter in which a witness was Jordan, parson of PIREFRICTH (facsimile in church). The grave of Stanley the explorer, is in the churchyard. *The Day before Yesterday - the story of Pirbright* Helen Yool

The **pump** just below Lock 1 of the Basingstoke Canal was installed in 2001. It sends water back above Lock 6 via a 30cm pipe under or beside the towpath, allowing the locks to function through Woking during water shortage - the most used part of the canal. Water shortage has always been a problem.

Richmond was the Manor of Sheen hived off from Domesday Book Kingston by Henry I. It was SCEON in a Saxon will of 950, probably derived from *Sheen* or *Shine* indicating beauty. Henry VIII changed the name to Richmond by decree in 1501. Edward I had made the manor house into a palace and it reached its apogee under Queen Elizabeth who died there. The palace was near the present Twickenham Bridge, where *Old Palace* appears in road names. The Old Deer Park stretched northwards from the palace beside the Thames where the name is still in use for the public sports fields. After the execution of Charles I, the buildings were quarried for use elsewhere and, though the site was later restored to the crown, the palace was not rebuilt. Richmond Lodge, near the Observatory in the Old Deer Park was a later Royal residence, also sometimes called a palace.

Richmond Bridge opened in 1777. James Payne was the architect; it cost £26,000. To be rowed there from London Bridge cost 1s 3d in 1828. Richard Yong was granted the ferry in 1442.

Richmond Hill is famous for its view and its place in poetry, painting and music. The Thames between Kew and Hampton Palace had drawn bigwigs to live beside it mainly because of its convenience for fast connection by boat to the various royal homes and other seats of power between Windsor and London. The parks of the rich adorned the Thames - recognized in the 18th century when conscious efforts were being made to beautify landscapes with noble buildings and fair gardens and became an additional reason for buying into it. In 1902, with London suburbs threatening to spread along the river, the view from Richmond Hill was protected by law (The Richmond, Ham and Petersham Open Spaces Act). The fountain at the top was installed by the RSPCA for horses labouring up the slope.

Richmond Lock and Weir, built 1894, are on the tidal Thames. They are only needed on the falling tide when steel barriers are lowered to maintain the river level upstream. After mid-tide these are drawn up and folded below the bridge.

Richmond Park was Sheen Chase of Henry VIII. Charles I bought adjacent land and made it into a hunting park in 1637. He hunted there in 1647 while awaiting trial. The Commonwealth gave it to the City of London who restored it to Charles II. It was opened to pedestrians in 1758 before hunting ceased. The 8 mile wall encloses 2358 acres/954 ha with Red & Fallow Deer. White Lodge has been the junior school of the Royal Ballet since 1955. It was built for George II in 1727 and subsequently became a residence for members of the royal family and prime ministers. Edward VII was incarcerated there with tutors to encourage his education. Edward VIII was born there. Pembroke Lodge is now a venue for weddings and conferences. It was built by George III for his "very good friend" the Duchess of Pembroke and was later granted to prime minister Lord John Russell whose grandson Bertrand grew up there. King Henry's Mound in the 12 acre garden is a barrow made into a belvedere.

Royal Parks - note for newcomers: Richmond, Bushy, Home and Windsor Great parks are closed at night, times varying with time-of-year. There are few public rights of way but numerous paths, tarmac, gravel and grass, as well as off-path walking. Some of the drives are used as public roads. Dogs must be under control because of the deer and are not allowed in the fenced gardens. Touching young deer causes them to be abandoned. Red deer stags should be treated with caution at the rut - in autumn.

St John's village grew around the wharf after the canal came through. The bridge got its name from a brick kiln. The Victorian Gothic church originated as a chapel-of-ease to (Old) Woking parish church in 1840 providing the name. St John's became a separate parish in 1883.

The **sandpit** in Horsell Common is where *The War of the Worlds* starts (1898). The narrator sees a flash on Mars, from a friend's observatory in Ottershaw, then a large metal cylinder falls upon the Common. Travellers on the Woking and Chobham roads are attracted to the crater by the mass of spectators and zapped by ray gun. There were evidently few trees when H G Wells (1866-1946) lived in Woking.   *War of the Worlds* H G Wells Everyman 1993

The **Semaphore Tower** at Chatley Heath is open to the public in the afternoon at week-ends and Bank Holidays from mid-Mar -Oct (☎ 01372 458822). It was restored in 1989 and the signalling mechanism may be operated by visitors.

The arms slot into the mast when at rest. The tower is 60½ feet tall and was built in 1822 as part of the chain of semaphore or telegraph stations from the Admiralty to Portsmouth, prompted by the Napoleonic Wars. The adjacent stations were on Cabbage Hill to the NE and Pewley Hill, Guildford to the SW. A branch chain from Chatley Heath to Plymouth was abandoned in 1832, before completion. Its first station was a similar tower beside the church in Worplesdon. The other stations were either bungalows or 3 storey houses.

Shepperton appears as SCEPERTONE in SPELETORNE Hundred on the Middlesex folios of the Domesday Book. Westminster Abbey was Lord of the Manor but operated it as a normal manor with 17 villeins and a priest. The church, St Nicholas, on the river bank in the old village, was built in 1614 and had the oblong tower added around 1700. Next to it, the rectory is a 7-bay timber framed hall of about 1500 concealed by later wings and mathematical tiles. The 12th century church is known from a drawing and appears to have suffered from floods; medieval wills included money to pay for piles for it.

Shepperton Lock was constructed in an artificial cut in 1813. A weir had been taxed for 6s 8d in the Domesday Book presumably for its flash lock revenue. In 1293 the Bishop of London was taking tolls for a dam and sluice.

Staines Bridge was built by the sons of Rennie, the railway/canal engineer and opened by William IV in 1832, 200 yards upstream of earlier bridges. The Roman bridge was the first above London. A grant of oaks indicates there was a bridge in 1228. The new stone bridge of 1791 cracked, an iron bridge of 1803 failed and the iron bridge of 1807 was damaged by the Copper Horse in transit. To be rowed there from London Bridge cost 2s 6d in 1828. Barges passing under, up or downstream, paid 4d in 1774 - an iniquity, as the bridge was an obstruction to them. Tolls under & over ceased in 1871.

Stanley (1841-1904) of "Dr Livingstone, I presume" fame retired to Furze Hill in the parish of Pirbright. Illegitimate, he grew up in a Welsh workhouse, fought in the American civil war and became a *New York Herald* journalist. His great *coup* was the expedition to central Africa to find Livingstone who had been "lost" trying to establish that Lake Tanganyika was the source of the Nile; they met at Ujiji, November 1871. In a second expedition he continued Livingstone's work, following the Lualaba River down to the sea to find it was the Congo, not the Nile. When employed by the Belgian king to set up a chain of trading stations Stanley became the creator of the Congo (now Zaire) and a catalyst for the carve up of Africa by the European powers. Wielding a sledge-hammer brought him the African name *Bula Mutari* - smasher of rocks.

The Royal **Star and Garter** Home on Richmond Hill is a nursing home for disabled servicemen and women. It was set up by royal charter in 1916 under the aegis of the Red Cross specifically for young men returning from the WWI front. The previous building was the Star & Garter Hotel but the present one was purpose built in 1928 under the architect Sir Edwin Cooper. For some patients it provides temporary rehabilitation, for others, a life-long residence.

Tagg's Island was bought as a base by Fred Karno in 1917 but was a "flop" because of World War I. He devised music hall burlesques and sent out teams of comics to perform them, bringing to light Stan Laurel, Wee Georgie Wood, Charlie Chaplin, Max Miller, etc.

Tank Hill, like the other hills near the M3 is capped by ice-age plateau gravels. Permission to fly model aircraft first appears in the 1935 minutes of Chobham Common and the knolls are the spiritual home of several clubs. *Tank Factory* was local vernacular for the military research station north of the present M3 started in 1942 when Chobham Common was requisitioned for testing tanks. It went on to devise technology and test for all sorts of fighting land vehicles.

Teddington is best known for its locks, the presence of NPL and large TV studios formerly Warner Bros Studios then Thames Television and now part of Pinewood. Noel Coward spent his early years in Teddington. People who lived there were Stephen Hales FRS 1677-1761 an early physiologist; R Blackmore, 1825-1900, author of *Lorna Doone* and Benny Hill, 1925-92. The impressive French Gothic Church, St Alban's, b1887, replaced the old church, St Mary's, when outgrown by the population of the faithful. The position is now reversed.

Teddington Lock is the official tidal limit of the river. It was first built in 1811 on the Teddington bank and rebuilt on the Ham side in 1858; removal of the old London Bridge had caused the water to fall to lower levels. There are three locks, the one opened in 1904 being the largest on the river, 650 feet long to take a tug with a string of 6 barges. Across the upper gate is seen the launch lock and the skiff lock. Two fish ladders are visible at the town end of the weir.

Thames Lock, at the outlet of the Wey Navigation, is manned because it is the toll collecting point and because the third gate sometimes has to be used. This was added in the 1820s when the Navigation was extended downstream to reach deeper water after Shepperton Lock lowered the Thames water level.

The Thames **Towpath** was put together by the Thames Conservancy of 1751 to overcome the stranglehold of landowners. At Ham Meadows the towpath disappeared because of erosion of the river bank. Barge owners had legal battles with Lord Dysart to pass through his land. Building a wooden walkway in the river was considered. From 1672 the barge carters paid a collective £8 p.a. but when the agreement terminated Lord Dysart charged 3d per horse and collected £81 in the first year, 1752. On the rising tide barges could float or be rowed upriver and bargees sustained the pubs while waiting for the tide to change. From 1850 the City of London (owners of the rights to the river) paid £105 p.a. and this was continued by the Thames Conservancy 1895-1898.

Trigg's Lock on the Wey Navigation is at a point where the river and canal re-join. The lock-keeper's main function is to regulate the water levels with the sluices. Formerly he would have collected tolls. The house bears a fire mark.

Twickenham Bridge designed by Maxwell Ayrton, opened in 1933 to carry the Chertsey Road.

Walsham Gates on the Wey Navigation are sited where the canal and river separate and are used as a lock only at flood times to prevent excessive flow in the canal. The turf sided lock is primitive - not lined with masonry.

Walton-on-Thames was the Domesday Book manor of WALETONE. A timber-framed gable of the Tudor manor house can be seen from the river. The first bridge opened in 1750 of timber braced arches; it is known from a painting of Canaletto. The later bridge of stone and brick opened in 1780. Turner painted this bridge by moonlight. Pevsner comments that only a contractor would be prepared to paint the iron third bridge of 1864. At the time of writing a new bridge is expected to replace the temporary iron girder road bridge of 2000. The Bailey bridge beside it for pedestrians was the WWII replacement for the Victorian iron bridge. The crossing was freed of tolls for £7000 in 1870. To be rowed to Walton Bridge from London Bridge cost 1s 9d in 1820.

West End expanded in the 19th century from a hamlet in the administrative west half of Chobham Parish. Gordon's School is there. It has had its own church, Holy Trinity from 1890 and became an ecclesiastical parish in 1895.

The River **Wey** has two main tributaries, each called Wey, the northern one rising at Alton and the southern from many springs near Haslemere and Selborne. The confluence is at Tilford. The main river runs from there via Godalming to Guildford, where the Cranleigh Water and Tilling Bourne join. It then skirts past Old Woking on its way to join the Thames at Weybridge.

The **Wey Navigation** from Weybridge to Guildford was made by improving the river bed and making cuts - the first long artificial waterway in Britain. Caen stone in the arches of Pyrford church (Norman) suggests the river was already in use for transport. The Navigation was approved by Act of Parliament in 1651 but the instigator, Sir Richard West of Sutton Place, had already cut a loop off the river in his grounds and built a lock at Stoke (juxta Guildford) around 1620, further development being delayed by the Civil War. The 15½ route miles are 9 miles of canal segments between stretches of the river with 12 locks. The last private owner, Harry Stevens, off-loaded the Navigation on the National Trust in 1964 but commercial use persisted between Tilbury Docks and Coxes Mill until 1983.   *London's Lost Route to the Sea* P A L Vine 1973 David & Charles 267pp

Weybridge was WAIGEBRUGG in a boundary list attached to the Saxon charter of 673 endowing Chertsey Abbey, presumably taking its name from a predecessor of the present iron bridge. In the Domesday Book it is WEBRUGE in AMELEBRIGE Hundred and is now part of Elmbridge Borough. In 1463 Thomas Warner obtained a license for a wharf at the mouth of the Wey.

Wisley, a synonym for the Royal Horticultural Society garden, is an ancient village on the banks of the River Wey north of the garden, WISELEI in the Domesday Book. When the sewage works were built, signs of neolithic and Iron Age habitation were found with a quernstone and 5 pottery kilns. The church of around 1140 retains its original form though the roof and some of the windows have been replaced. Points of interest: chalk chancel arch, Norman windows, gothic windows of 1627, Elizabethan hour glass bracket over pulpit, the sarsen by the door which probably caused the church to be sited here.

Wisley Airfield opened during WWII to test aircraft from the nearby Vickers' factory at Brooklands, including the Wellington bomber. Its potential is said to have been spotted by a test pilot, "Mutt" Summers, who crash landed on the farmland in the 1930s. It was used for prototype trials, engine testing, kitting out and storage of aircraft and had workshops and test sheds. The runway, grass until 1952, saw the initial flights of the Viking, Viscount, Valiant, Vanguard, BAC-111 and VC10. Brian Trubshaw's autobiography gives a lively account of the airfield in use. Large aircraft were towed from Brooklands along the A3 on Sunday nights. Heathrow's development and proximity was one of the reasons for the British Aircraft Corporation closing it in 1973.

Surrey Airfields in the Second World War 1997 Len Pilkington Countryside Books

The **Wisley Garden** of the Royal Horticultural Society (0143 224234) opens every day except Christmas. The inaugural meeting of the society was in 1804 after an initial suggestion from John Wedgewood (son of Josiah) to William Forsyth, gardener of George III. The garden started as 1½ acres in South Kensington but transfered to a 33 acre site in Chiswick in 1823 and was soon actively searching in China and North America for new plants. The royal charter was awarded in 1861. The Wisley site was a 60 acre private garden started in 1878. Sir Thomas Hanbury bought it as a gift for the RHS in 1903 "for the purpose of an Experimental Garden and the Encouragement and Improvement of Scientific and Practical Horticulture in all its branches". The timber framed lab was completed in 1916 and the first head of research was Prof Fred Keeble. More land has been acquired so the area of the garden is now 240 acres.   *Wisley - The Royal Horticultural Society's Garden* M & A Rix 1989

Old **Woking** was the village of WOCHINGES manor in the Domesday Book, a large royal estate with church and mill. Granted away by King John, it reverted to the crown through inheritance. The manor house became Woking Palace. The church, St Peter, was founded around 675, according to a papal letter of 710, the first record of Woking. It was a cell of the monks of Medeshamstead, now called Peterborough. The oldest parts of the present building are the Norman west and north walls of the nave. The door which now opens into the base of the tower of 1200 has been dendrochronologically dated to around 1050. Points of interest: replacement windows of the nave, 1350, next to the Zouche gallery; east window around 1350; mid-15th century oak pews; 15th & 17th century chests; Purdan brass 1523; Shadan brass 1527.

Woking mushroomed in the 19th century. The canal was operating by 1796 and the railway by 1838 but did not cause growth for the land was Common which could not be sold. An Act of Parliament in 1852 enabled the Necropolis Company to buy 2600 acres of Woking Common for Brookwood Cemetery, most of which was sold for building. Small parcels were sold to numerous builders, houses rose higgledy piggledy on the heath tracks and there was no urban authority, hence the chaotic roads. Woking did not become an Urban District Council until 1895. Modern councils have done well to give Woking a centre and through ways.   *A History of Woking* Allan Crosby 1982 Phillimore 224pp

Woking Mill is probably on the site of the Domesday Book mill. Until 1835 it supplied flour for London, made from wheat bought at the Guildford market then it became a paper mill which had 136 workers in 1870. Unwin Brothers bought it when they were displaced by fire from their mill at Chilworth in 1896 and added the Dutch gables. Three turbines drove the machinery and water still spews from three conduits under the building. The site was being redeveloped for residential use at the time of going to print.

Woking Palace was a favoured home of Henry VIII, many letters being signed there. It was set in a deer park, three miles in circumference, stretching north-wards. It is said Wolsey heard of his elevation to cardinal while visiting. Edward VI and Queen Elizabeth I used it. In 1620 James I granted the manor to Edward Zouche who took the stone for his new house, Hoe Bridge Place, in the village. The moat is still visible and a grey outbuilding which would have been used for storage is still standing.
          The Ruins of Old Woking Palace D J Haggard *Surrey Archæological Collections* vol 55 1958